PIANO Adventures®

by Nancy and Randall Faber

THE BASIC PIANO METHOD

______________________ is sightreading this book!
(your name)

Production Coordinator: Jon Ophoff
Cover: Terpstra Design, San Francisco
Illustrations: Erika LeBarre

ISBN 978-1-61677-638-1
Copyright © 2013 Dovetree Productions, Inc.
c/o FABER PIANO ADVENTURES, 3042 Creek Dr., Ann Arbor, MI 48108.
International Copyright Secured. All Rights Reserved. Printed in U.S.A.
WARNING: The music, text, design, and graphics in this publication are protected
by copyright law. Any duplication is an infringement of U.S. copyright law.

CHART YOUR PROGRESS

SIGHTREADING

SIGHTREADING SKILL

Good sightreading skill is a powerful asset for the developing musician. It makes every step of music-making easier. With the right tools and a little work, sightreading skill can be developed to great benefit.

In language literacy, the reader must not only identify single words, but also group words together for understanding. Similarly, music reading involves more than note naming. The sightreader tracks horizontally and vertically, observing intervals and contour while gleaning familiar patterns that make up the musical context.

As students begin sightreading with eighth notes, several systems of counting are used, each of which may support the others. They are:

- traditional metric counting (1 + 2 + 3 + 4 +)
- counting with rhythm syllables (ta, ta, ti-ti ta,)
- counting using words (walk, walk, run-ning walk)

As students begin sightreading with 5-finger scales, identifying the specific 5-finger scale of the piece is a first step. The 5-finger scales used within a set of five exercises are often varied to keep students on their toes!

The decoding skill of sightreading requires repetition within familiar musical contexts. In other words, pattern recognition develops by seeing a lot of the same patterns. This book offers carefully composed variations to sharpen perception of the new against a backdrop of the familiar. Consistent with the literacy analogy, the musician must not simply identify single notes, but also group notes into meaningful musical patterns.

How to Use

This book is organized into sets of 5 exercises, for 5 days of practice. Each set provides variations on a piece from the **Piano Adventures® Level 2A Lesson Book (2nd Edition).** Play one exercise a day, completing one set per week.

Though the student is not required to repeatedly "practice" the sightreading exercise, each should be repeated once or twice as indicated by the repeat sign. For an extra workout, play each of the previous exercises in the set before playing the new exercise of the day.

Curiosity and Fun

The "Don't Practice This!" motto is a bold statement which has an obvious psychological impact. It reminds us that sightreading is indeed "the first time through" and it reminds us to keep the activity fun.

The comic-style illustrations ("educational art") draw students through consecutive pages by stimulating curiosity. Little Treble, Little Bass, Penny Piano, Freddie Forte, Buddy Barline and other characters captivate the beginning reader with musical questions, antics, and requests. Each page presents a new "learning vignette" in a spirit of fun.

Level of Difficulty

It is most beneficial to sightread at the appropriate level of difficulty. Some experts say that a child should not stumble on more than three or four words per page when learning to read. Similarly, a sightreader should not stumble on more than three or four notes per page. This Piano Adventures® Sightreading Book is carefully written to match the Level 2A difficulty and to provide appropriate challenge.

Marking Progress

Students are encouraged to draw a large **X** over each completed exercise. This instruction is so out of the ordinary that students find it immensely satisfying to mark their progress in this way.

DON'T PRACTICE THIS!

Additionally, students wishing to celebrate the completion of a set may color the illustration of Day 5.

Some students may exclaim about the thickness of the book! They soon are rewarded to find how fast they can move through it. Indeed, with confidence increasing, the student can take pride in moving to completion of this very large book…and do so with a crescendo of achievement.

Instructions to Student

1. Scan the music before playing.
2. Play the music without stopping.
Always repeat, then cross it out.
3. Play one exercise a day.

I'm Freddie Forte.

Hi, I'm Chord Guy, your sightreading guide.

I'm Little Bass.

I'm Little Treble.

After sightreading, put a BIG X across the music... Go ahead!

DAY 1: When the Saints Go Marching In

DON'T PRACTICE THIS!

1 3
mf
Oh, when the notes go march-ing in,
3 1

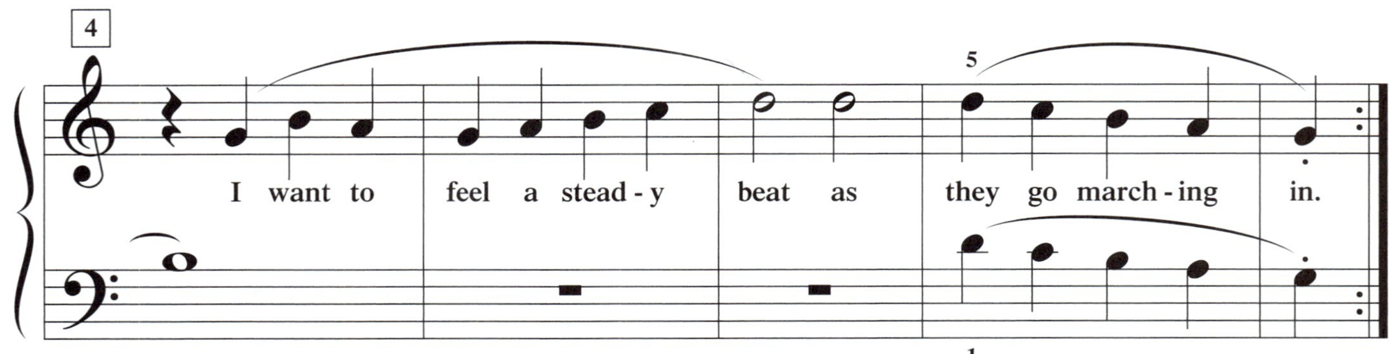
4
5
I want to feel a stead-y beat as they go march-ing in.
1

DAY 2: When the Saints Go Marching In

DON'T
PRACTICE
THIS!

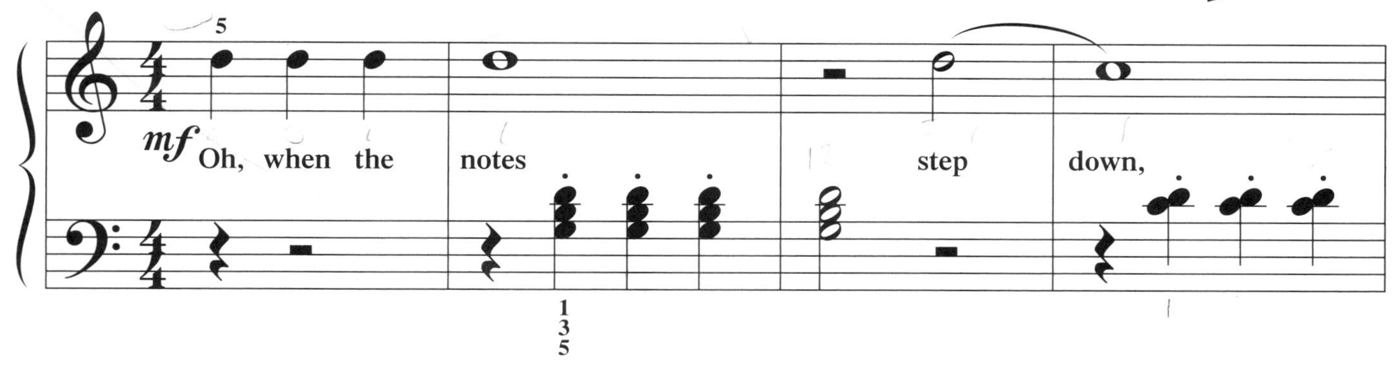
5
mf
Oh, when the
notes
step
down,
1
3
5

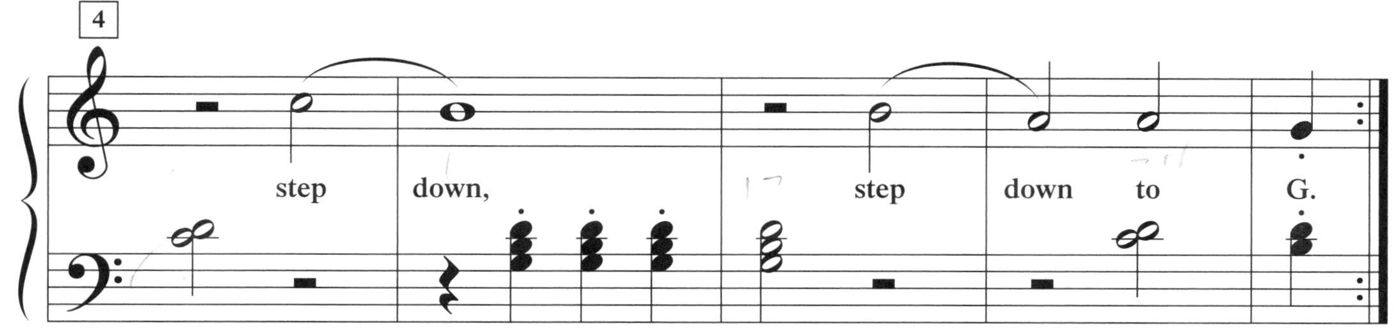
4
step
down,
step
down to
G.

RHYTHM ROAD
Ex. 1 2 3 4
Write the counts 1 2 3 4 for Rhythm Road.
Clap or tap and count aloud!
Shhh. Quiet, please! I'm Penny Piano.
Ting! Ting!

DAY 3: When the Saints Go Marching In

DON'T PRACTICE THIS!

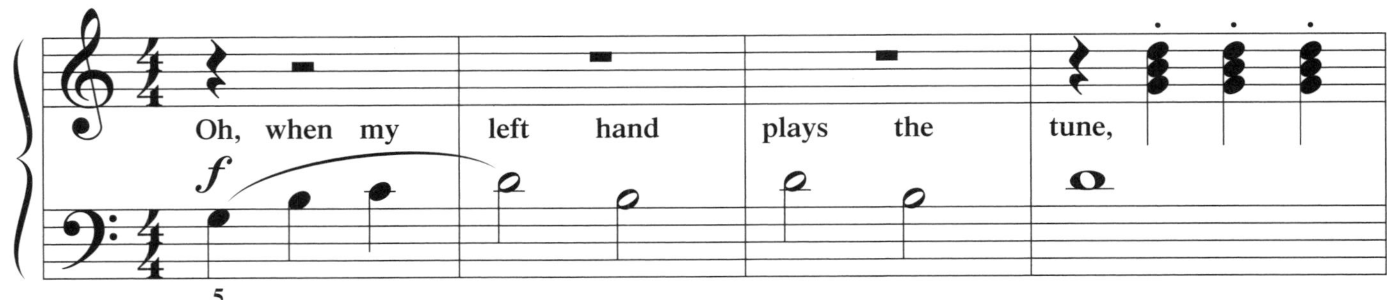
Oh, when my left hand plays the tune,

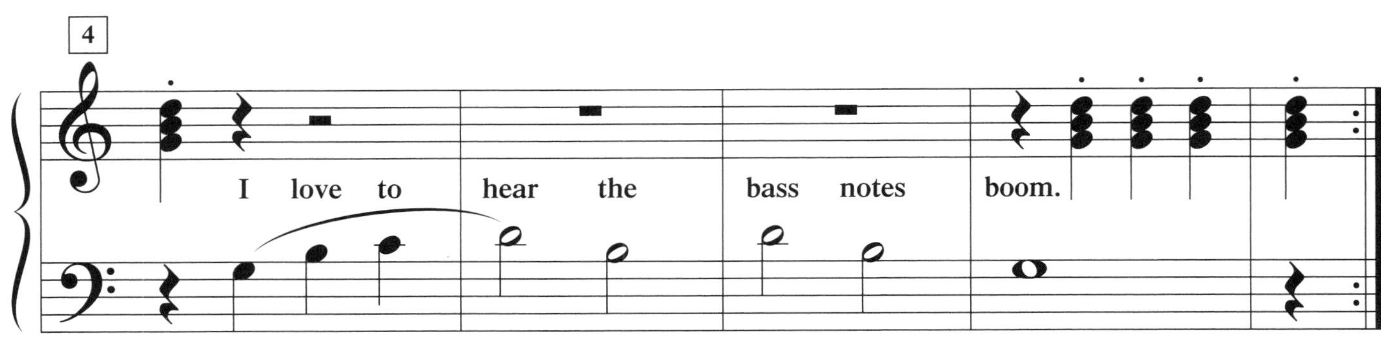
4
I love to hear the bass notes boom.

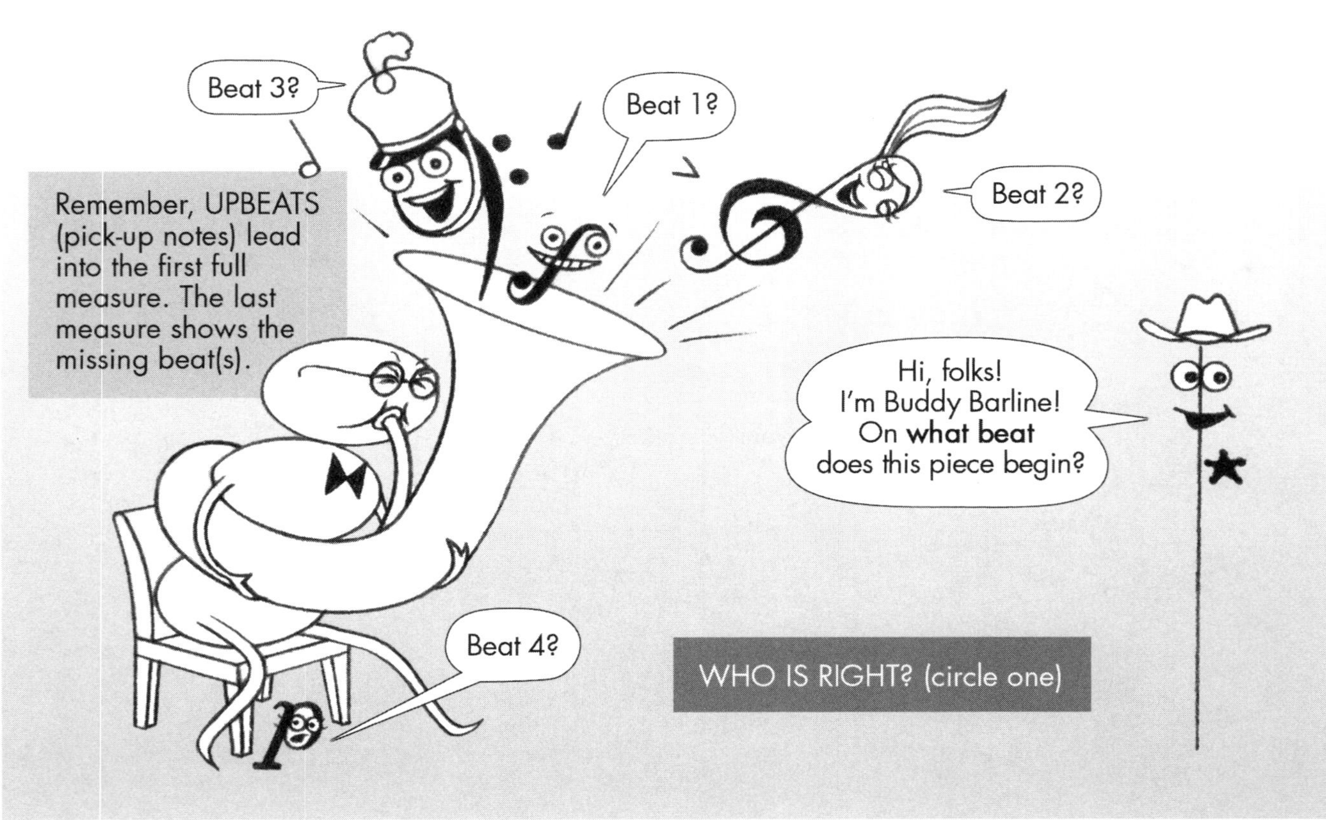
Beat 3?
Beat 1?
Beat 2?
Remember, UPBEATS (pick-up notes) lead into the first full measure. The last measure shows the missing beat(s).
Hi, folks! I'm Buddy Barline! On **what beat** does this piece begin?
Beat 4?
WHO IS RIGHT? (circle one)

DAY 4: When the Saints Go Marching In

DON'T PRACTICE THIS!

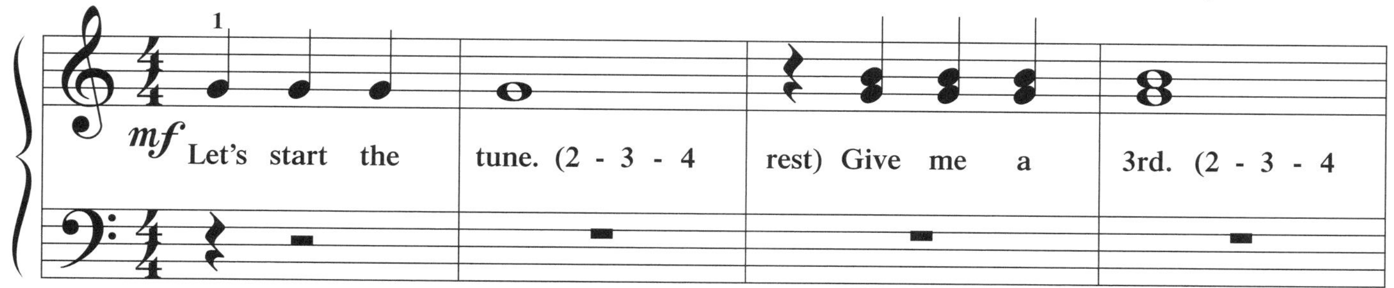
1
mf
Let's start the
tune. (2 - 3 - 4
rest) Give me a
3rd. (2 - 3 - 4

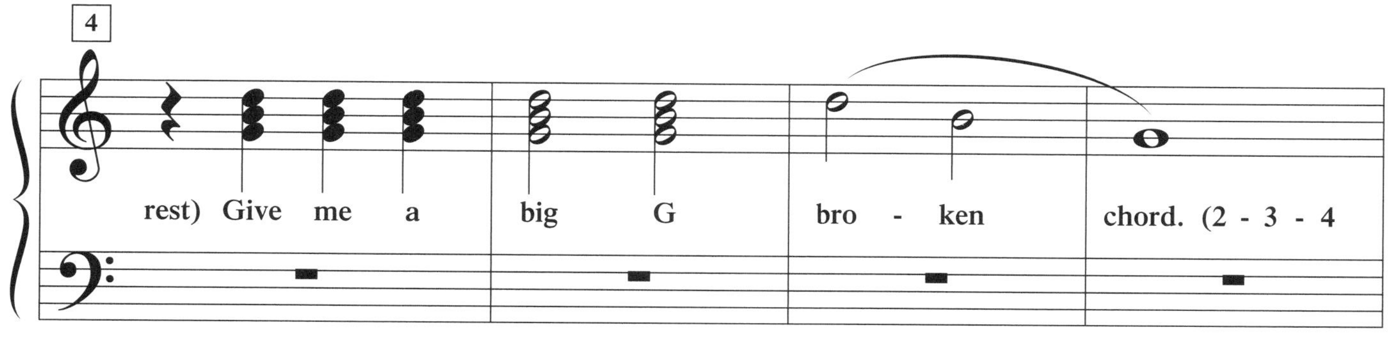
4
rest) Give me a
big G
bro - ken
chord. (2 - 3 - 4

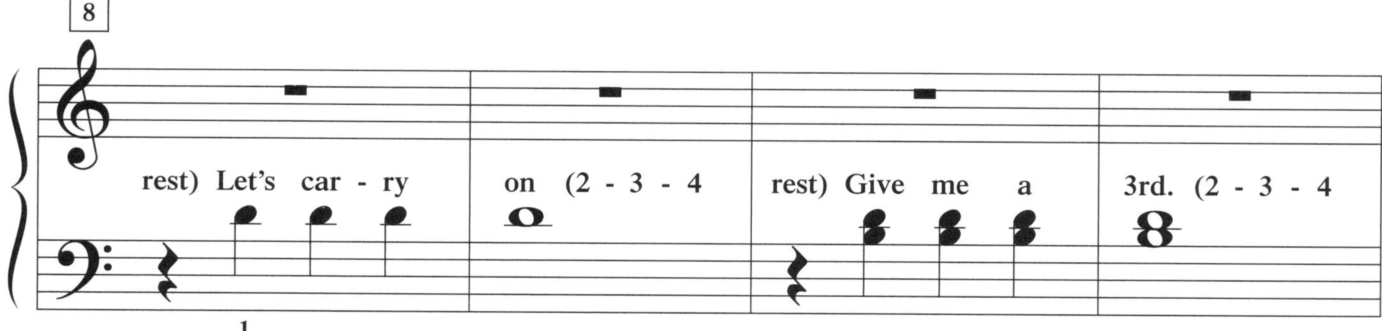
8
rest) Let's car - ry
on (2 - 3 - 4
rest) Give me a
3rd. (2 - 3 - 4
1

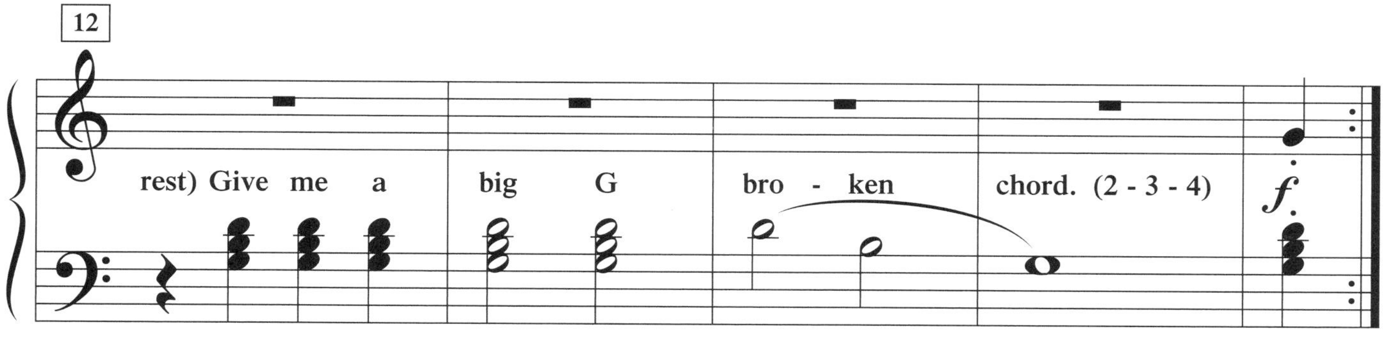
12
rest) Give me a
big G
bro - ken
chord. (2 - 3 - 4)
f

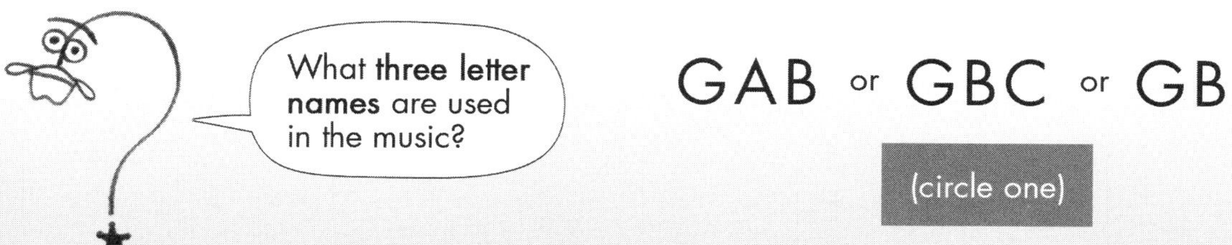
What three letter names are used in the music?

GAB or GBC or GBD

(circle one)

Name each interval in the hats below!
Let's march! HUP-2-3-4!

DAY 5: When the Saints Go Marching In

DON'T PRACTICE THIS!

3rd

5 3

mf Oh, when the saints go march - ing in,

1

4

they might just skip and skip a - gain.

8

5

And as they step and sing this song,

WOW! You made it to DAY 5! We applaud you!
Put a big X across the music.
Ting!
Ting!

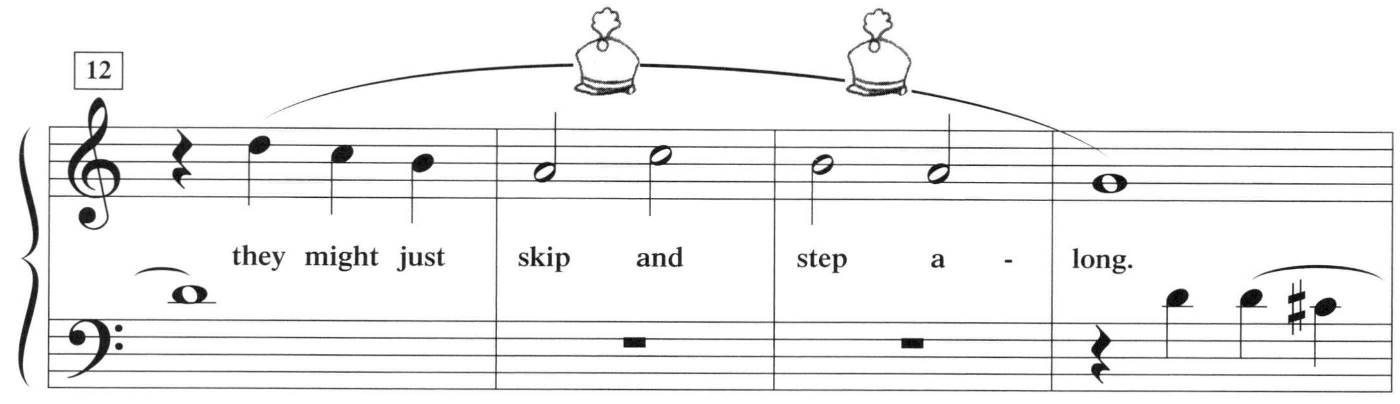
12
they might just skip and step a - long.

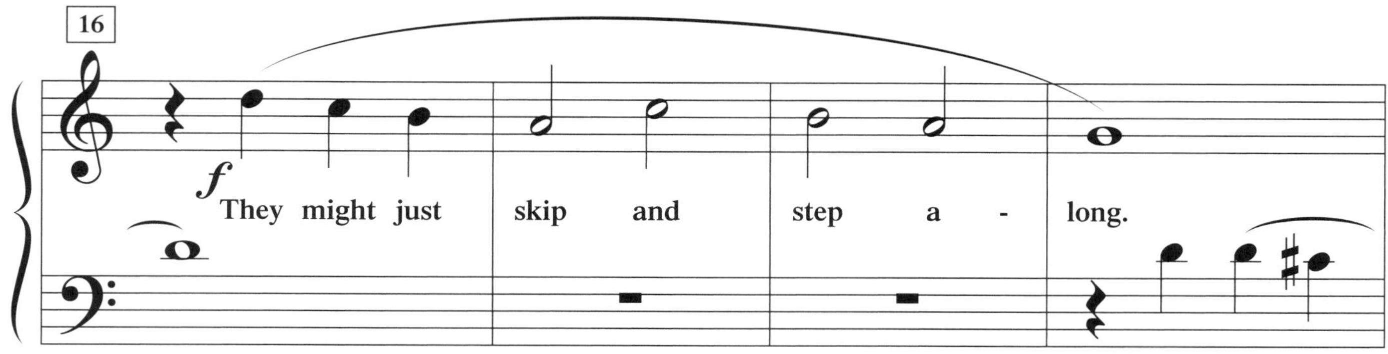
16
f
They might just skip and step a - long.

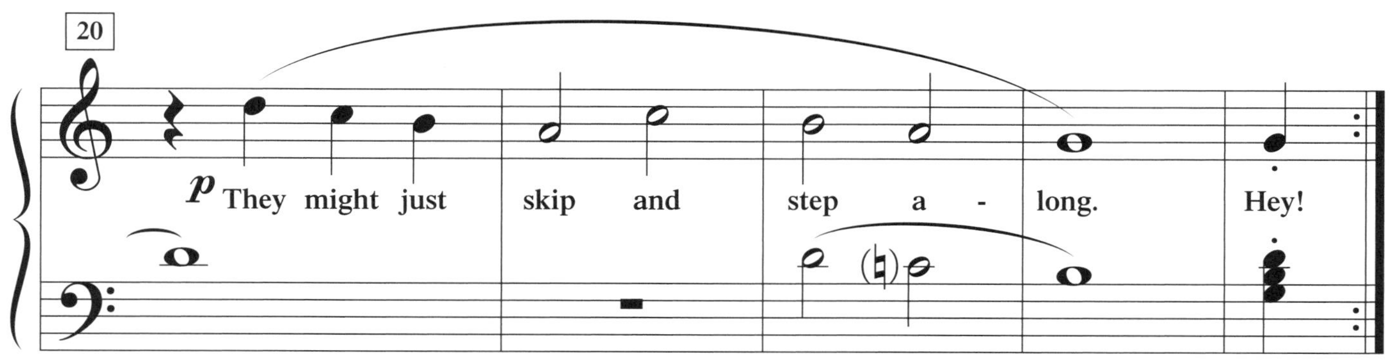
20
p
They might just skip and step a - long. Hey!

DAY 1: Famous People

Jack + Sophie

DON'T PRACTICE THIS!

Notice the starting finger numbers.

3
Guess who this is?
He's a fa-mous per - son.
He flies, he flies,
3

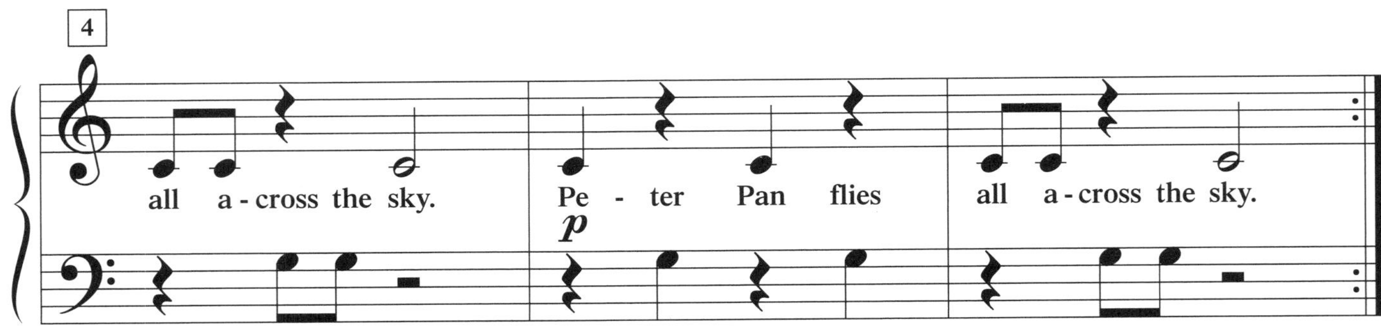
4
all a - cross the sky.
Pe - ter Pan flies
all a - cross the sky.

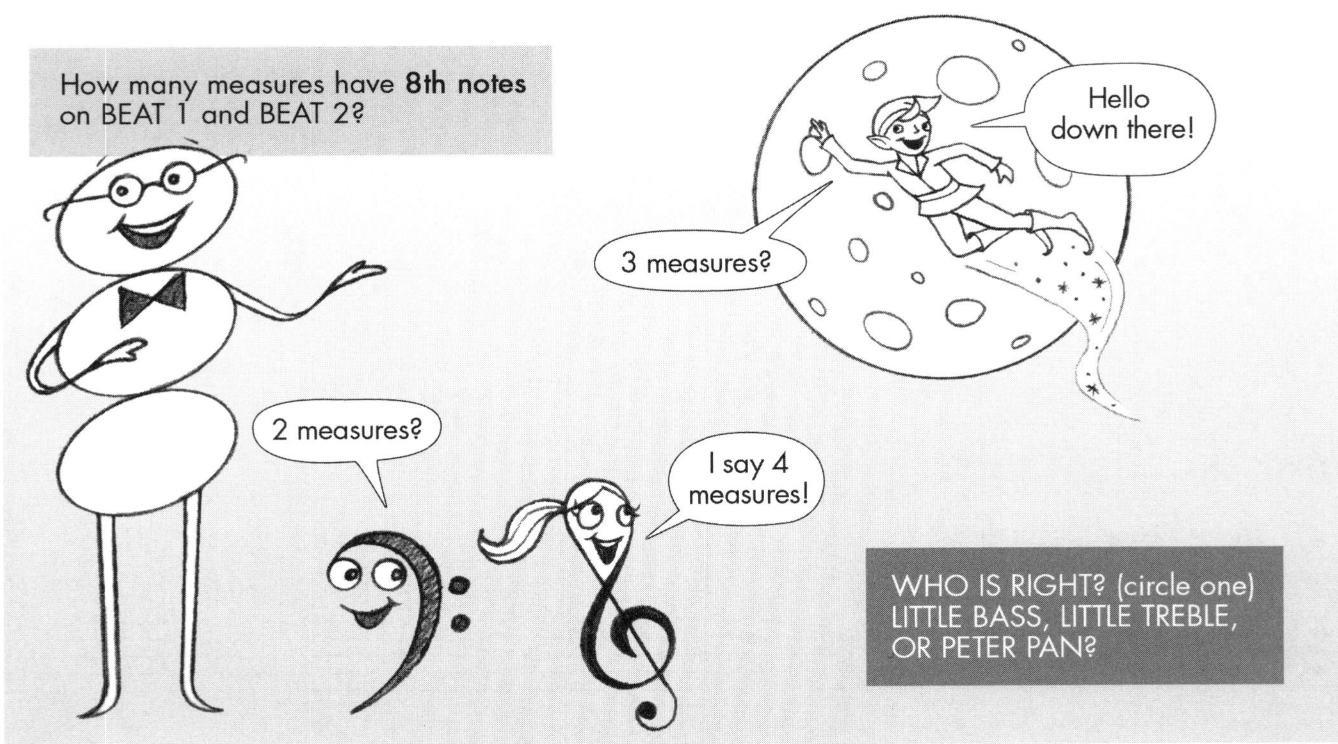
How many measures have **8th notes** on BEAT 1 and BEAT 2?
Hello down there!
3 measures?
2 measures?
I say 4 measures!
WHO IS RIGHT? (circle one) LITTLE BASS, LITTLE TREBLE, OR PETER PAN?

RHYTHM ROAD
1
Write the counts 1 2 3 4 for Rhythm Road.*
Sure thing!
Achoo!

DAY 2: Famous People

DON'T PRACTICE THIS!

Name the 5-finger scale ____

1
mf
Do you know this girl? She is fa - mous, too! Lit - tle Red Rid - ing Hood,
1

4
Lit - tle Red Rid - ing Hood. Met a wolf but she was saved, lived to play an - oth - er day!

*The teacher may ask the student to write 1 + 2 + 3 + 4 +.

DAY 3: Famous People

_____ 5-Finger Scale

DON'T
PRACTICE
THIS!

mf
Do you know this
ver - y fine com-pos - er?
Do you know this

4
ver - y fine com-pos - er?
Lud-wig van Bee-thov - en,
Lud-wig van Bee-thov - en.

DAY 4: Famous People

f
Mo-zart and Hay-dn are
fa - mous com - pos - ers,
fa-mous com - pos - ers.
p
RHYTHM ROAD
PUT AN X THROUGH EACH INCORRECT MEASURE

DAY 5: Famous People

______ 5-Finger Scale

DON'T
PRACTICE
THIS!

1
Let's name fa - mous peo - ple.
How 'bout Fred - die For - te?
Pe - ter Pan and Chord Guy,
f
5
4
Lit - tle Pen - ny Pian - o.
5
Lit - tle Red Rid - ing Hood
5
run - ning home just like she should!
1

I'm famous in all kinds of music!
CONGRATULATIONS! You made it to DAY 5! Can you name each "famous character" below?
All pianists know me!
I'm loud and famous!
BEETHOVEN
I'm swirly and famous!
Shhh...

DAY 1: Skip to My Lou

______ 5-Finger Scale

DON'T PRACTICE THIS!

See Chord Guy below about the missing bar lines!

mf
Who is Lou, Lou, Lou? Who is Lou, Lou, Lou?
5
Who is Lou, Lou, Lou? Skip to my Lou, my Lou, Lou, Lou!
Draw bar lines after every 4 beats.
Write the intervals in the violins above. (2nd, 3rd, 4th, 5th)

1. HOW MANY MEASURES USE THIS RHYTHM PATTERN? ____
2. WHICH MEASURE USES A SLUR? measure ______
Answer these questions about my fiddle music.
The answers are at the bottom of the page.

DAY 2: Skip to My Lou

______ **5-Finger Scale**

DON'T PRACTICE THIS!

3

p Skip to my Lou, ta ti - ti ta, skip to my Lou,

1
5

4

ta ti - ti ta, skip to my Lou, ta ti - ti ta,

7

f step - ping down the street.

① 2

Skip to my Lou.

Answers: 1. seven 2. measure 7

quarter rest
half rest
whole rest

quarter rest
half rest
whole rest

quarter rest
half rest
whole rest

Good sightreaders know RESTS. Circle the **correct name** for each rest.

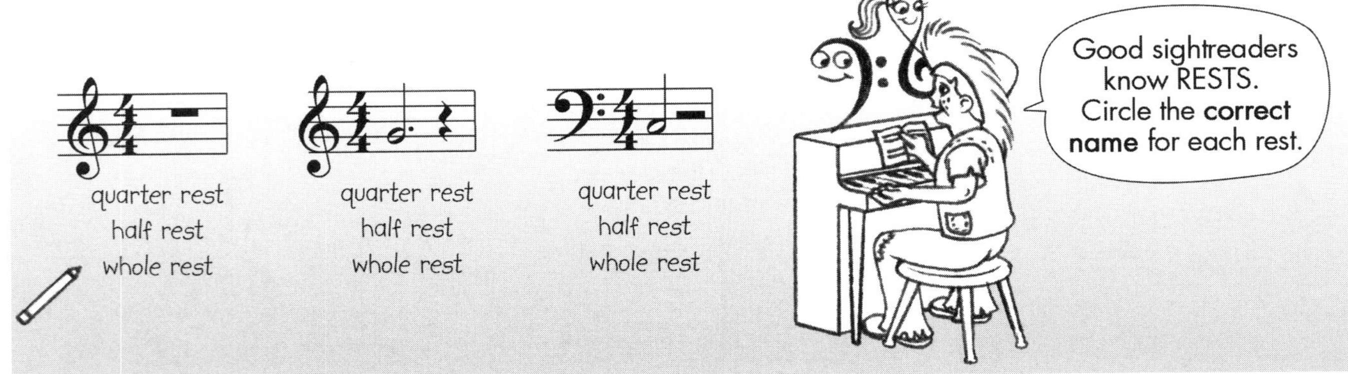

DAY 3: Skip to My Lou

_____ **5-Finger Scale**

DON'T PRACTICE THIS!

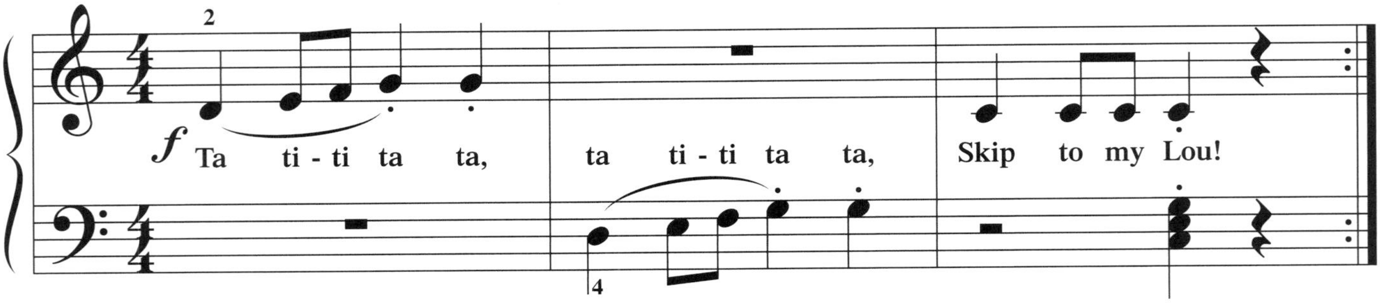
2
f Ta ti - ti ta ta, ta ti - ti ta ta, Skip to my Lou!
4

DAY 4: Skip to My Lou

_____ **5-Finger Scale**

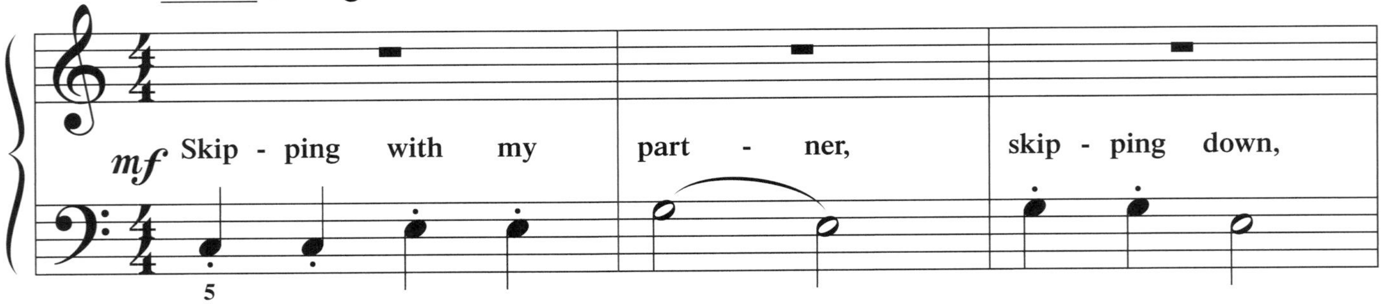
mf Skip - ping with my part - ner, skip - ping down,
5

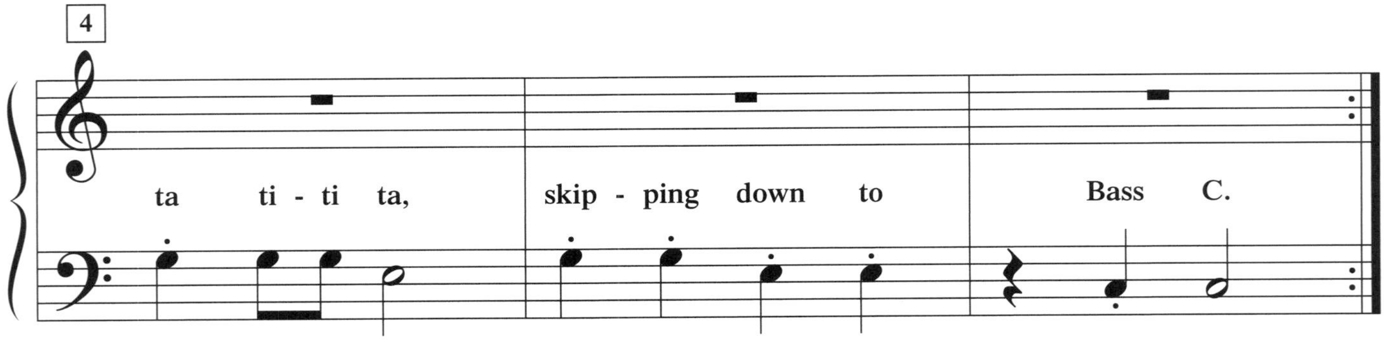
4
ta ti - ti ta, skip - ping down to Bass C.

DAY 5: Skip to My Lou

______ 5-Finger Scale

DON'T PRACTICE THIS!

See Little Red Riding Hood below about the rests!

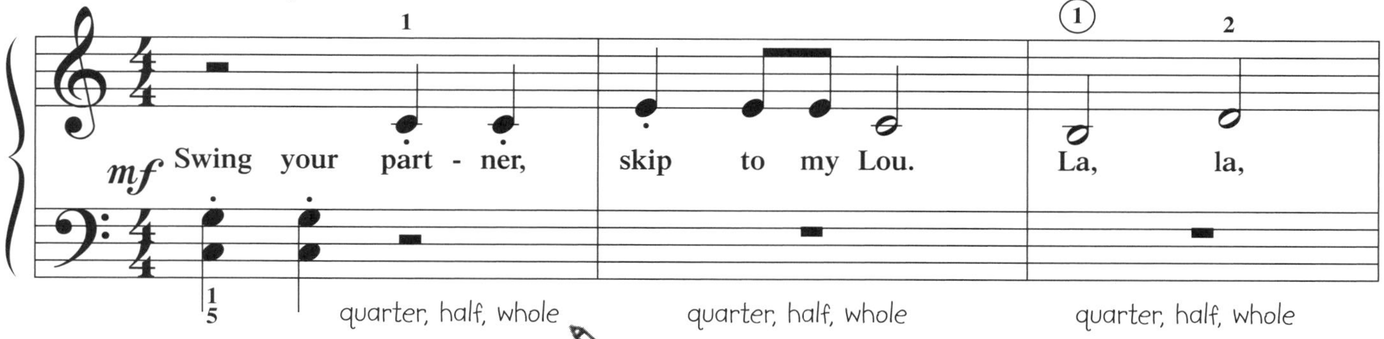

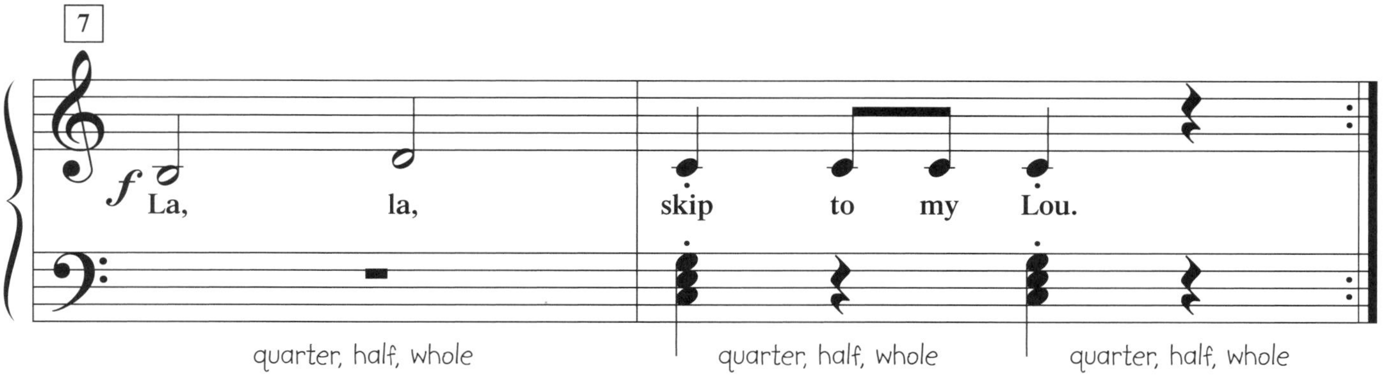

mf Swing your part - ner, skip to my Lou. La, la,

quarter, half, whole quarter, half, whole quarter, half, whole

4

la, la. Swing your part - ner, skip to my Lou.

quarter, half, whole quarter, half, whole quarter, half, whole

7

f La, la, skip to my Lou.

quarter, half, whole quarter, half, whole quarter, half, whole

Way to go!

Circle the **rest** used in each measure above.

Great! You made it to **DAY 5**!

La La

DAY 1: A Minuet for Mr. Bach's Children

Jael & Sophie

DON'T PRACTICE THIS!

2
mp
Jo - hann Bach
loved the min - u - et.
3
1

3
Ta ta ta
ti - ti - ti - ti ta.

A minuet is always in 3/4. What does 3/4 mean?
Hooray! Mr. Bach is teaching today!
3 beats in a measure. The ♩ note gets 1 beat.
No! 3 beats in a measure. The ♩ note gets 3 beats.
BACH
WHO IS RIGHT? (circle one)

Musical greetings! Before sightreading, add **bar lines** to this little minuet. Then play!
BACH

DAY 2: A Minuet for Mr. Bach's Children

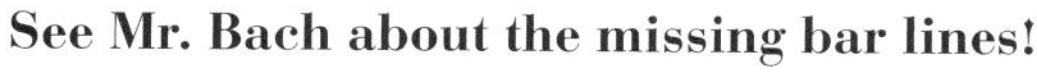
DON'T PRACTICE THIS!

See Mr. Bach about the missing bar lines!

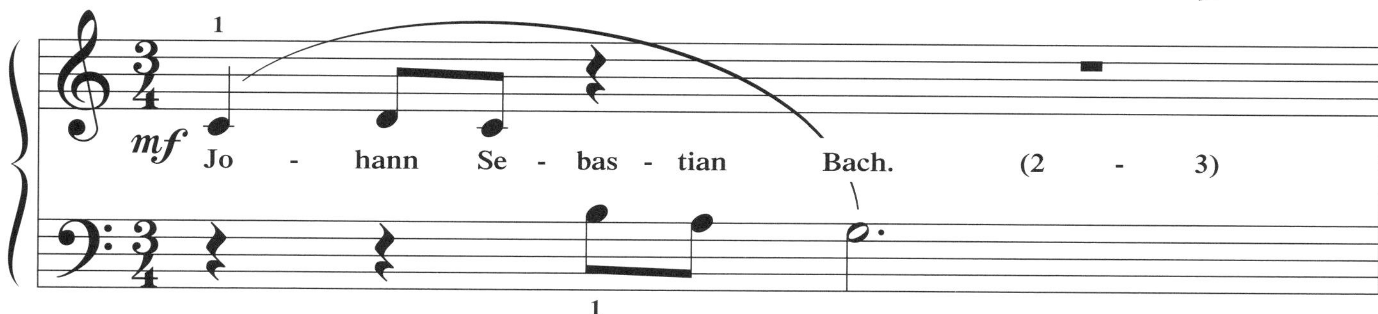
1
mf
Jo - hann Se - bas - tian Bach. (2 - 3)
1

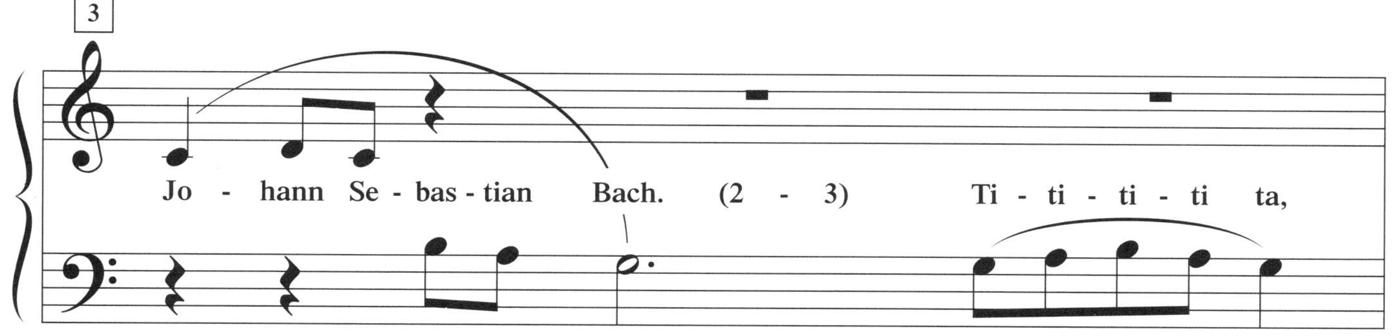
3
Jo - hann Se - bas - tian Bach. (2 - 3) Ti - ti - ti - ti ta,

6
ti - ti - ti - ti ta, Jo - hann Se - bas - tian Bach. (2 - 3)

DAY 3: A Minuet for Mr. Bach's Children

DON'T
PRACTICE
THIS!

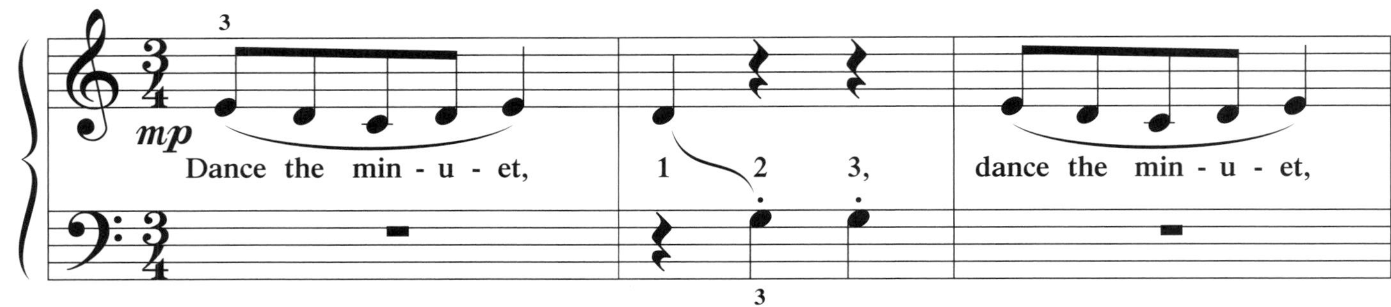

mp
Dance the min - u - et,
1 2 3,
dance the min - u - et,

4
1 2 3.
Dance the min - u - et,
1 2 3,

7
give a curt - sy and a
bow. (2 - 3)
How many measures use this pattern?
3 measures!
4 measures!
WHO IS RIGHT?
(circle one)

C♯
F♯
G♯
Name the sharp used. (circle)
BACH

DAY 4: A Minuet for Mr. Bach's Children

DON'T PRACTICE THIS!

Notice the starting fingers.

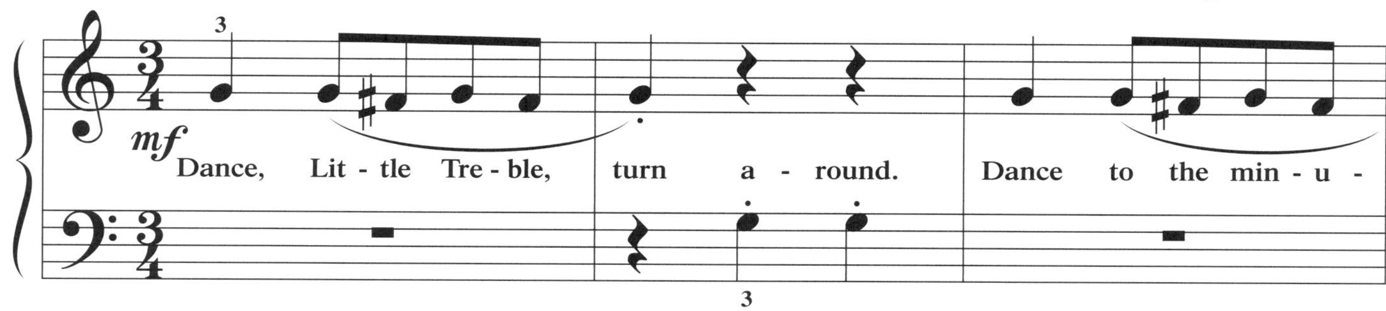
3
mf
Dance, Lit - tle Tre - ble, turn a - round. Dance to the min - u -
3

4
et. (2 - 3) Fred - die For - te, Pen - ny Pian - o,
f
p

7
mf
all dance the min - u - et. Take a bow! (2 - 3)
3
1
3

G
R
E
BACH
A
T

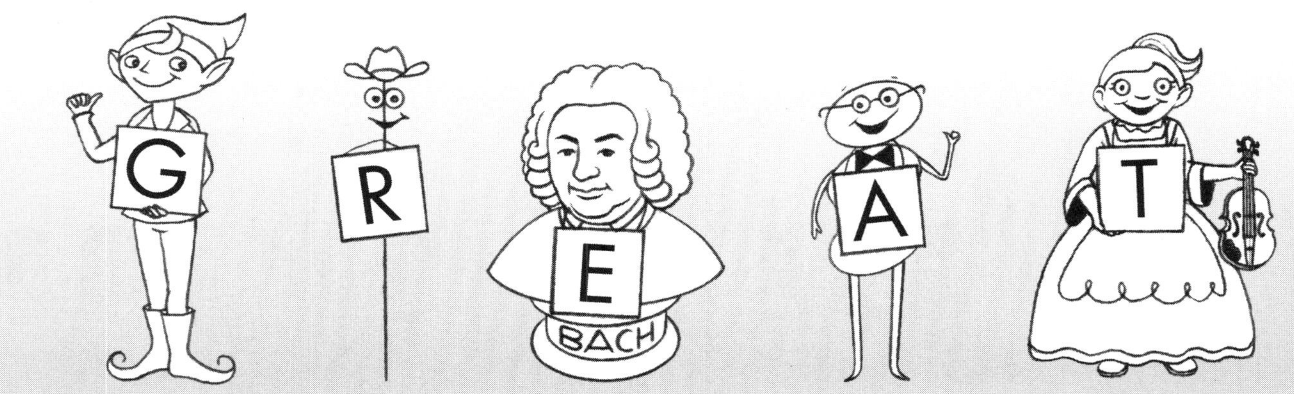

DAY 5: A Minuet for Mr. Bach's Children

DON'T PRACTICE THIS!

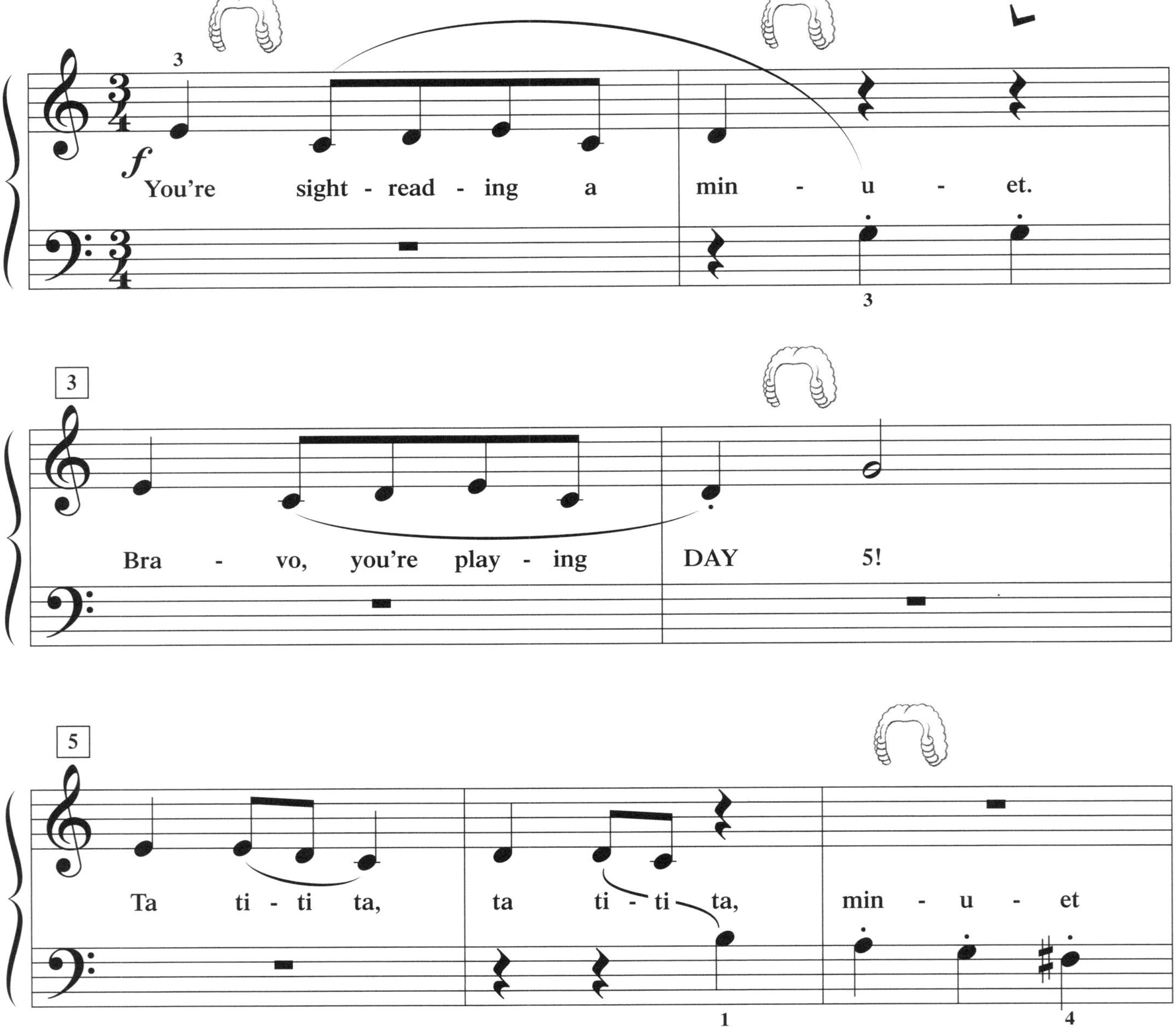
3
f
You're sight - read - ing a min - u - et.
3
3
Bra - vo, you're play - ing DAY 5!
5
Ta ti - ti ta, ta ti - ti ta, min - u - et
1
4

Write the intervals inside each wig.
W
O
R
K

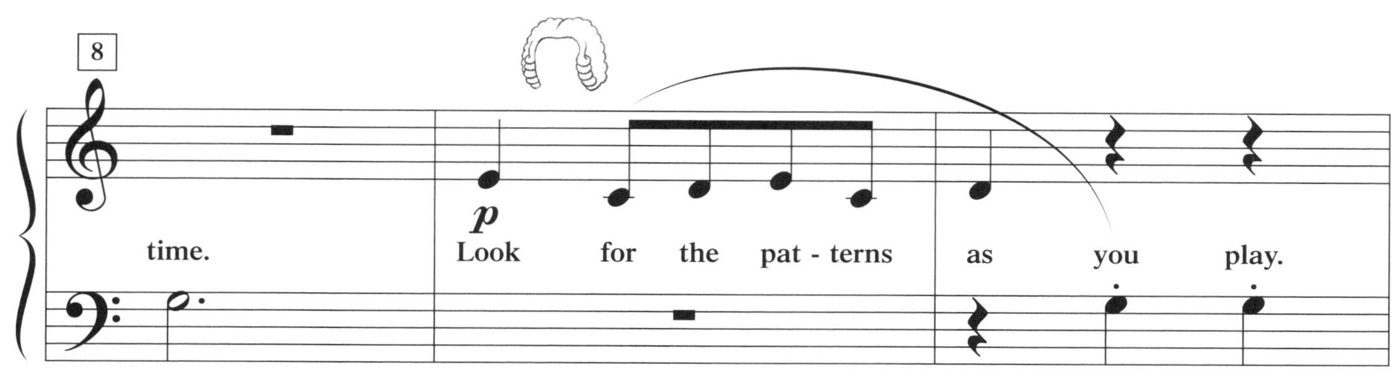
8
p
time.
Look for the pat - terns
as you play.

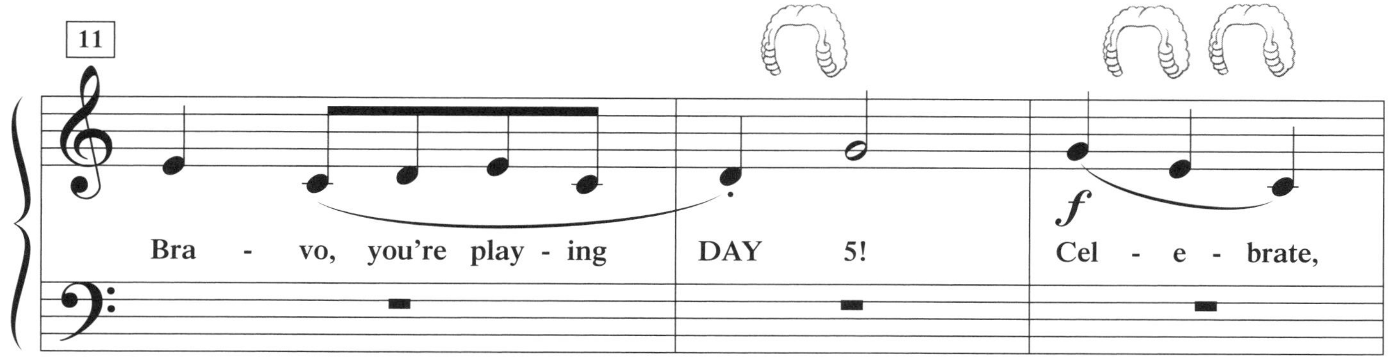
11
f
Bra - vo, you're play - ing
DAY 5!
Cel - e - brate,

14
sight - read - er,
we're clap - ping for
you.
1
4

DAY 1: Ice Cream

______ 5-Finger Scale

DON'T PRACTICE THIS!

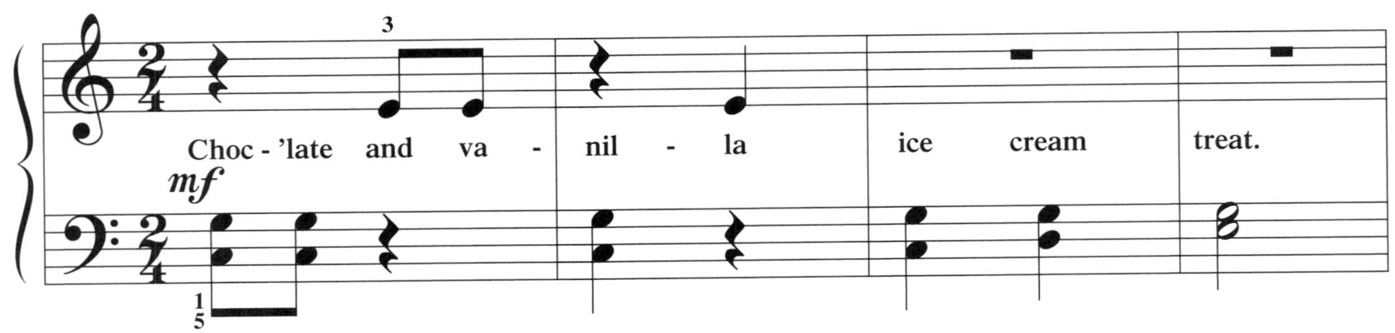
3
Choc - 'late and va - nil - la ice cream treat.
mf
1
5

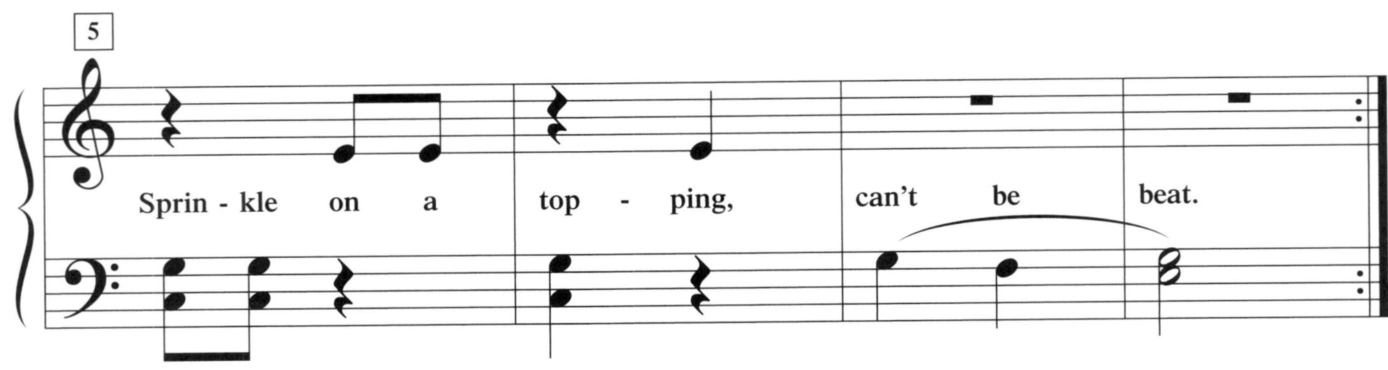
5
Sprin - kle on a top - ping, can't be beat.

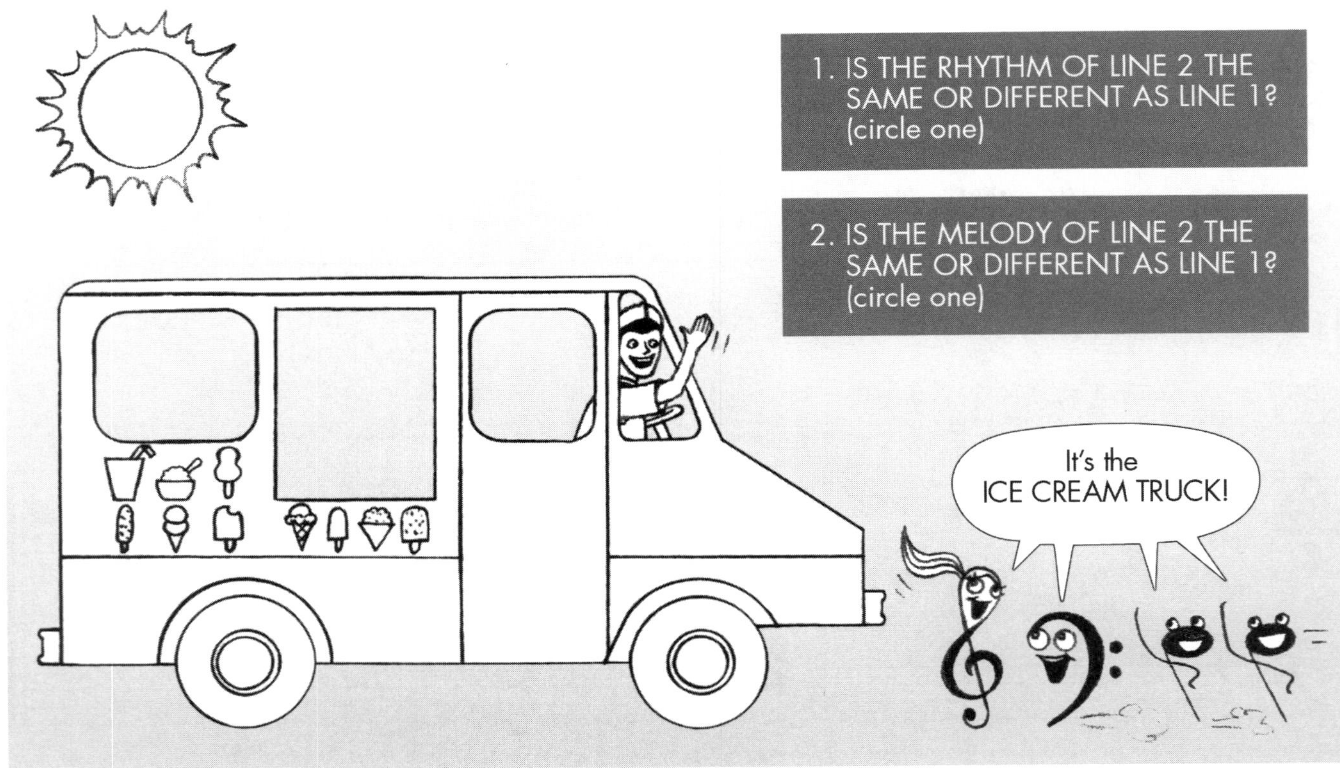
1. IS THE RHYTHM OF LINE 2 THE SAME OR DIFFERENT AS LINE 1? (circle one)
2. IS THE MELODY OF LINE 2 THE SAME OR DIFFERENT AS LINE 1? (circle one)
It's the ICE CREAM TRUCK!

staccato
forte
accent
piano
DRAW A LINE CONNECTING THE MATCHING TREATS.

DAY 2: Ice Cream

DON'T PRACTICE THIS!

_____ 5-Finger Scale

f Let's get some ice cream! Let's get some ice cream!

mf I like choc' - late. *f* Let's get some ice cream!

DAY 3: Ice Cream

_____ 5-Finger Scale

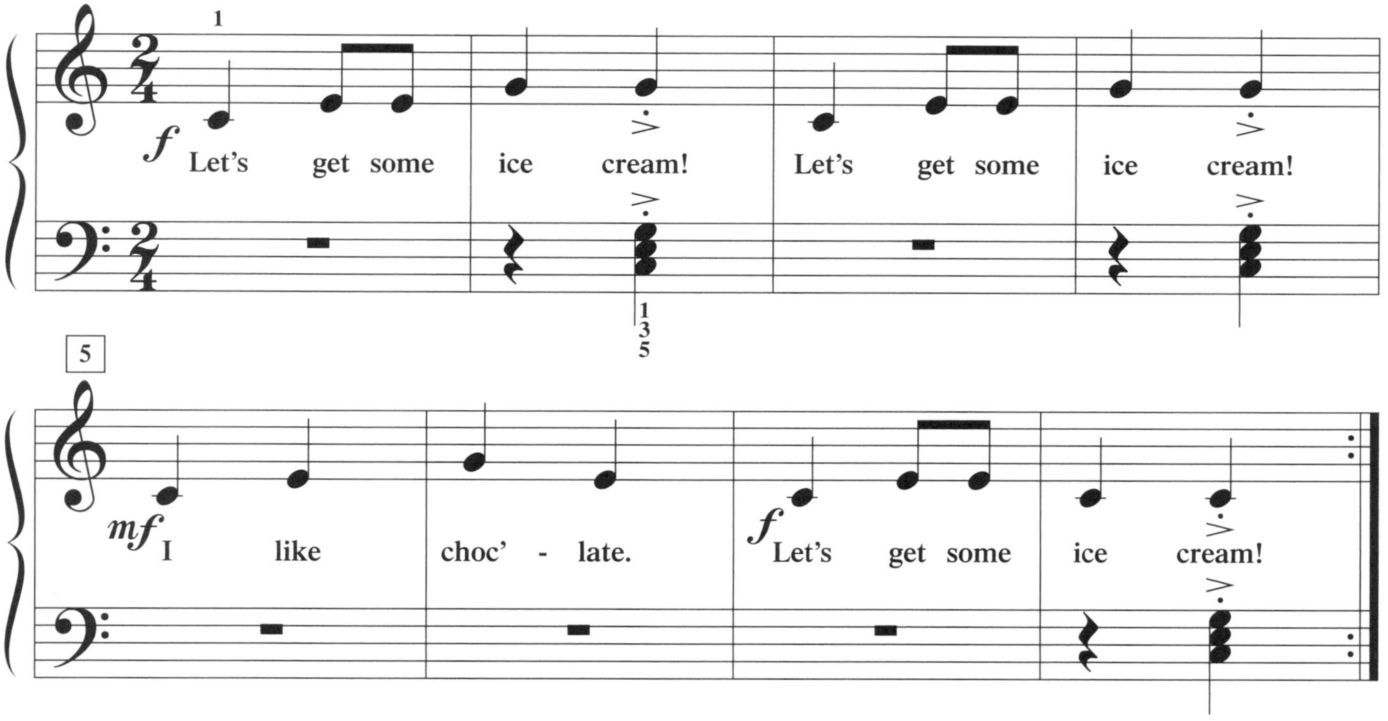

I'd like ice cream served at lunch, break - fast, din - ner, and at brunch!

DAY 4: Ice Cream

_____ **5-Finger Scale**

DON'T
PRACTICE
THIS!

1
f
Ice cream's great on pies we bake! Ta ta ti - ti ta.
1
2

5
2nd
p
Ice cream's great on birth - day cake! Ta ta ti - ti ta.

9
mf
In my tum - my, ice cream's yum - my!
1
4

Write the interval in each cake.
Wait for me!

2 measures!
HOORAY FOR YOU!
4 measures!
DAY 5!
HOW MANY MEASURES USE 3RDS? (circle one)
3 measures!

DAY 5: Ice Cream

______ 5-Finger Scale

DON'T PRACTICE THIS!

5
mf If I had a lit - tle luck, I would own an ice cream truck.
1
5

5
In the sum-mer, it would go to the neigh-bor - hoods I know.

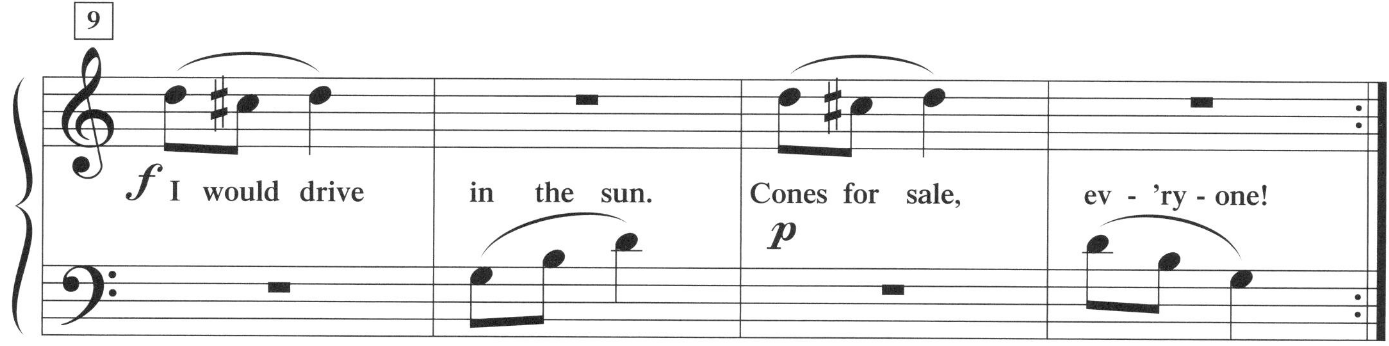
9
f I would drive in the sun. Cones for sale, ev - 'ry - one!
p

DAY 1: My Daydream
_____ 5-Finger Scale
DON'T PRACTICE THIS!
B
mp
Chirp - ing, chirp - ing, chirp - ing, chirp - ing,
Day - dream - ing, lis - t'ning to all the birds sing.
After sightreading, write the note name in each cloud above.

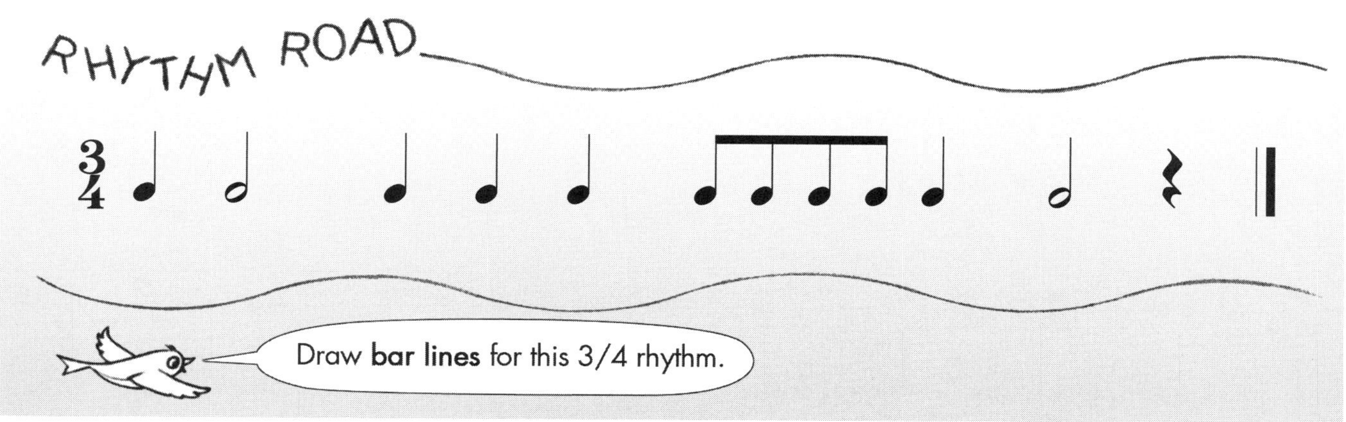
RHYTHM ROAD
Draw **bar lines** for this 3/4 rhythm.

DAY 2: My Daydream

_____ **5-Finger Scale**

DON'T PRACTICE THIS!

mp Sun's out, blue skies,

1
3
5

5

day - dream, in the grass - y green field. (2 - 3)

9

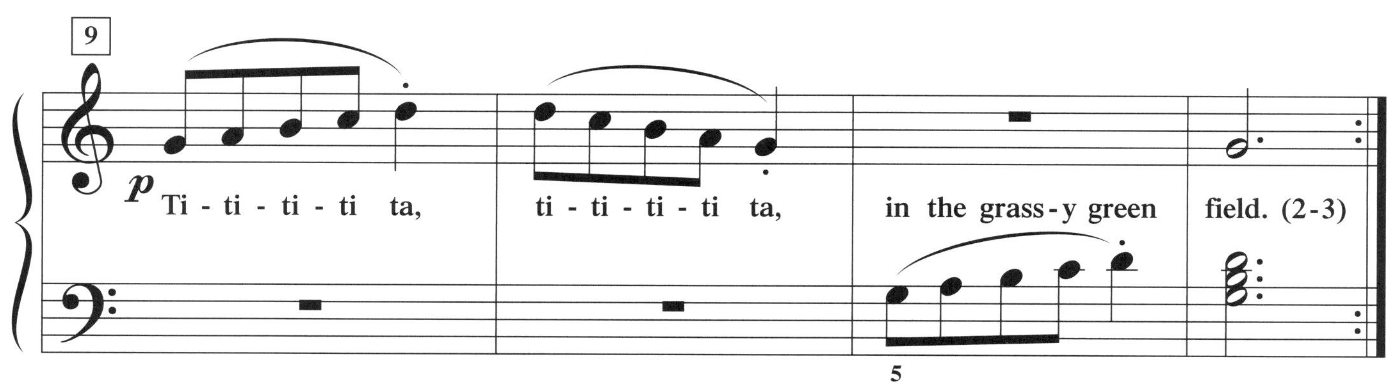
p Ti - ti - ti - ti ta, ti - ti - ti - ti ta, in the grass - y green field. (2-3)
5

DAY 3: My Daydream

______ 5-Finger Scale

DON'T PRACTICE THIS!

mp
1
3
I love to day-dream. I'm fly - ing, fly - ing.

5
Up in the sky, I'd go fly - ing so high.

Ex.
Write the missing note to form a G chord in each cloud.

Hello,
flying friends!
How many measures
use only half steps?
4?
5?
6?
WHICH LITTLE BIRD IS CORRECT? (circle)

DAY 4: My Daydream

_____ 5-Finger Scale

DON'T
PRACTICE
THIS!

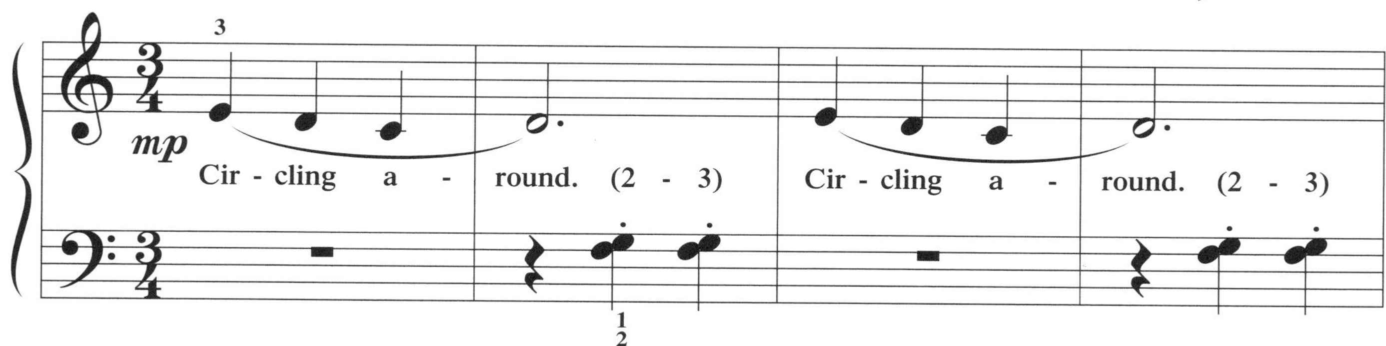
3
mp
Cir - cling a - round. (2 - 3) Cir - cling a - round. (2 - 3)
1
2

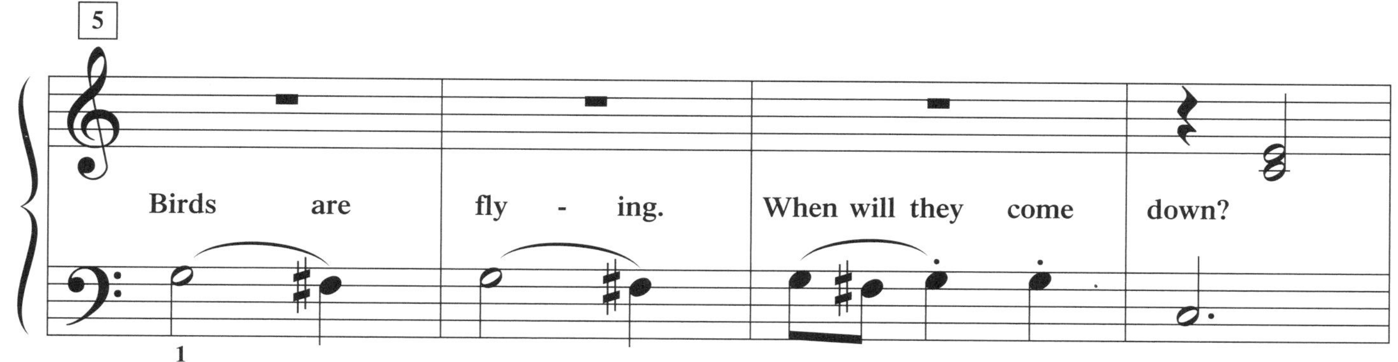
5
Birds are fly - ing. When will they come down?
1

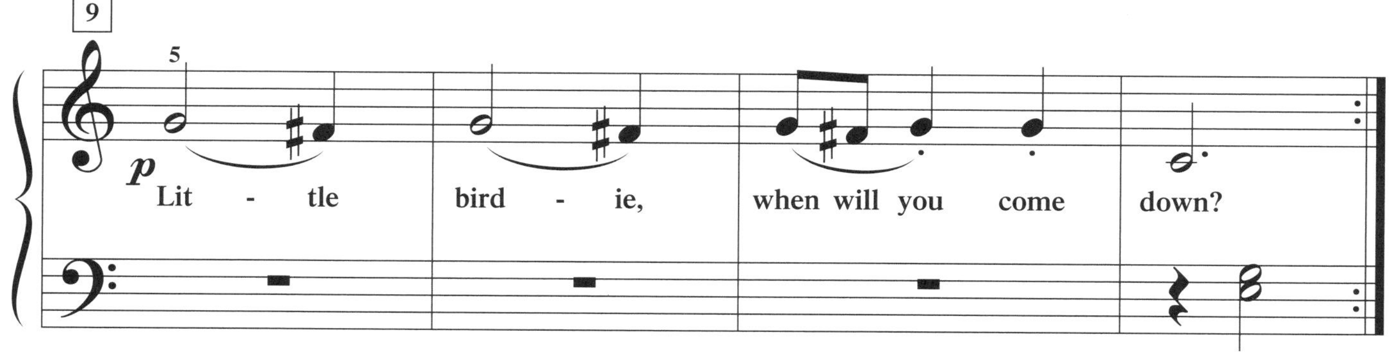
9
5
p
Lit - tle bird - ie, when will you come down?

DAY 5! GREAT JOB, SIGHTREADER!
IN YOUR DAYDREAM, WHERE WOULD
YOU GO? I'D BE...
Driving the
ice cream truck!
Sleeping...
In
Paris!

DAY 5: My Daydream

DON'T PRACTICE THIS!

_____ **5-Finger Scale**

3

I love to dream, (2 - 3) la la la la la la la, (2 - 3)

mf

1
3

5

3

la la la la la la la, (2 - 3) where I could be. (2 - 3)

9
Moun - tains for me, (2 - 3) la la la la la la la, (2 - 3)

Flying with Peter Pan!
Flying over the ocean!
Fiddling with my friends!
Playing in Carnegie Hall!
On the dance floor AND flying with Peter AND eating ice cream AND at Carnegie Hall!

13
4
la la la la la la
la, (2 - 3)
or by the
sea! (2 - 3)

17
4
Day - dream - ing
where I could
be.

I'll race you, Little Treble.
You're on!
There are 13 little clocks. Can you write the **note name** in each?

DAY 1: The Clock Strikes Thirteen!

DON'T PRACTICE THIS!

_____ 5-Finger Scale

Hold the damper pedal down throughout.

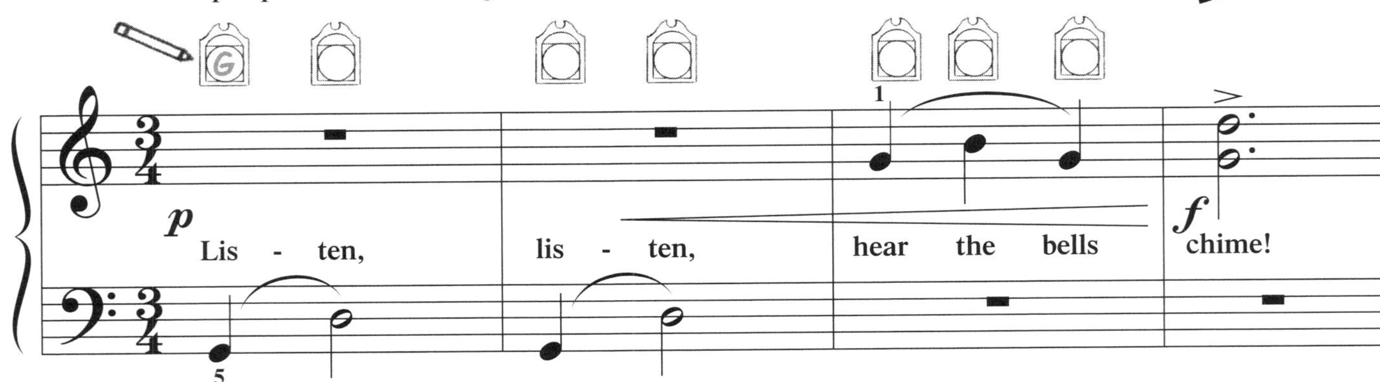
G
p
Lis - ten, lis - ten, hear the bells chime!
f

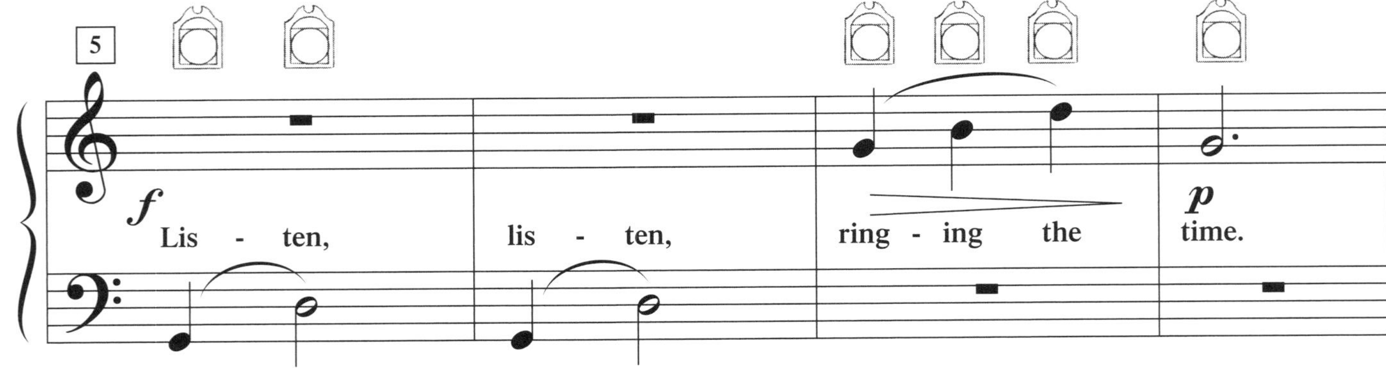
5
f
Lis - ten, lis - ten, ring - ing the time.
p

9
p
Ding, dong, ding, dong, ding, dong, ding!
rit.
f

DAY 2: The Clock Strikes Thirteen!

DON'T PRACTICE THIS!

_____ 5-Finger Scale

Hold the damper pedal down throughout.

1
f
Chimes ring
1 2 3,
ring out
1 2 3!
1
5
5
Chimes ring
1 2 3,
fade out
1 2 3.
p

DAY 3: The Clock Strikes Thirteen!

_____ 5-Finger Scale

Without pedal.

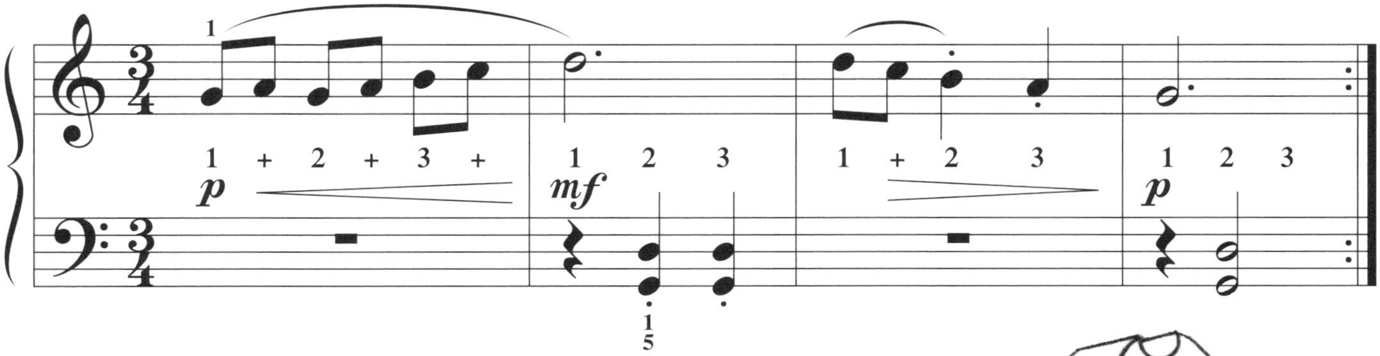

1

1 + 2 + 3 + | 1 2 3 | 1 + 2 3 | 1 2 3

p mf p

1
5

Name the five notes of the **G 5-finger scale**.

_____ _____ _____ _____ _____

Now name the five notes of the **C 5-finger scale**.

_____ _____ _____ _____ _____

Show you know! Fill in the blanks.

Penny and I are a GREAT team!
Shhh...
Write the note names in the bells below.

DAY 4: The Clock Strikes Thirteen!

_____ 5-Finger Scale

DON'T PRACTICE THIS!

Hold the damper pedal down throughout.

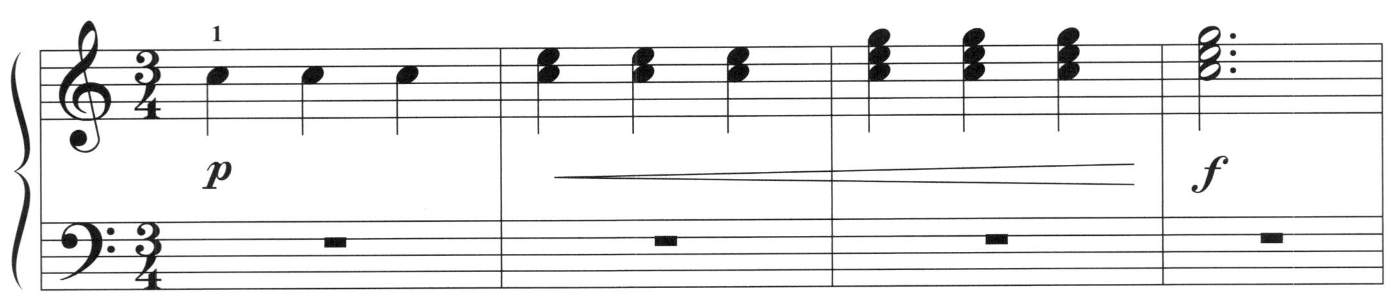

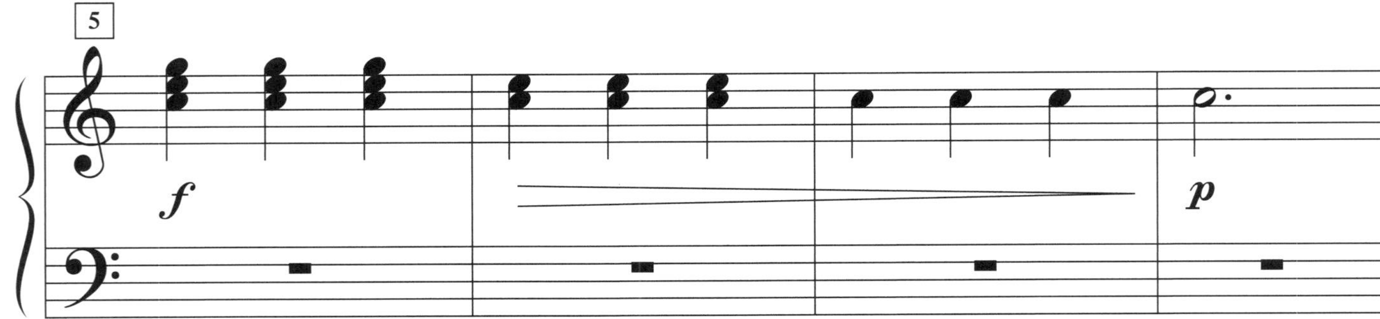

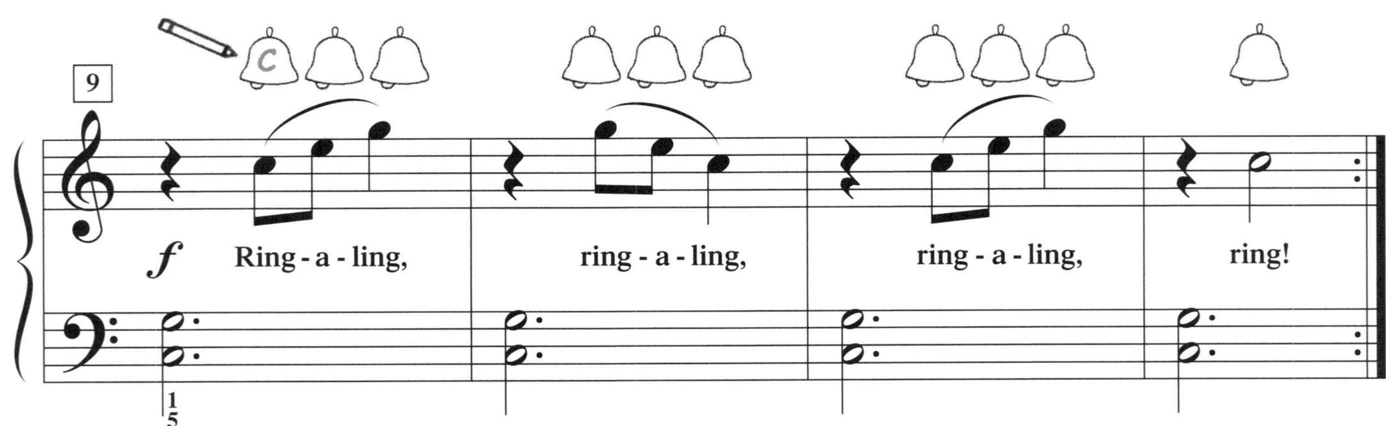
C
Ring - a - ling,
ring - a - ling,
ring - a - ling,
ring!

DAY 5: The Clock Strikes Thirteen!

_____ 5-Finger Scale

DON'T
PRACTICE
THIS!

Hold the damper pedal down throughout.

f Ring - a - ling - a - ling, ring - a - ling - a - ling, in the morn - ing.

5 Ring - a - ling - a - ling, ring - a - ling - a - ling, in the night.

9 *rit.* *p*

2nd • • B down to G

3rd • • E down to D

4th • • D down to G

5th • • D down to A

DAY 5! You're right on time! Connect these **intervals**.

DAY 1: Ode to Joy

_____ **5-Finger Scale**

DON'T PRACTICE THIS!

mp
Count: 1 2 3 4 | 1 2 3 - 4 | 1 2 + 3 4 | 1 2 3 - 4

5
mf

Guten Tag, young man. Can you answer these **musical questions**?
Beethoven is talking to me!!!
BEETHOVEN

1. What **scale** is being used?

   ____

2. What is the loudest **dynamic mark** above?

   ____

3. Which measure has **half rests**?

   ____

4. Which measure has the interval of a **3rd**?

   ____

Answers: 1. C scale 2. mf 3. measure 4 4. measure 7

Guten Tag, little friends! Is the music of Line 2 exactly the same as Line 1?
Yes, Mr. Beethoven.
No, Mr. Beethoven.
BEETHOVEN
WHO IS RIGHT? (circle one)

DAY 2: Ode to Joy

DON'T PRACTICE THIS!

_____ 5-Finger Scale

3 4 *mf* 1

5

3

9

2 *f* *p*

A hearty welcome, Mr. Bach! Please give us a musical challenge!
Certainly, Mr. Beethoven... Name the **highest note** in this piece!
Hmm, C?
Umm, G?
WHO IS RIGHT? (circle one)
BEETHOVEN
BACH

DAY 3: Ode to Joy

_____ **5-Finger Scale**

DON'T PRACTICE THIS!

Tap the rhythm of measures 1-2 before sightreading.

Count: 1 + 2 + 3 4 | 1 2 3 - 4

mf

5

mf

9

f *p* *mf*

DAY 4: Ode to Joy

DON'T PRACTICE THIS!
B
mp
5
9
Good sightreaders can find PATTERNS. Write each **note name** in the box. What pattern do you notice?
I want to do the treble notes!
I want to do the bass notes!
BEETHOVEN
WHAT SHOULD LITTLE TREBLE AND LITTLE BASS NOTICE?

Congratulations, Sightreader! Celebrate what you know!
Circle two of me in the music.
BEETHOVEN
I'm improving with rhythm. How about you?
DO THE 8TH NOTES FOR DAY 5 FALL ON BEAT 1, 2, 3, OR 4? (circle one)

DAY 5: Ode to Joy

______ 5-Finger Scale

DON'T PRACTICE THIS!

Count: 1 2 3 4 | 1 2 3 4 | 1 2 + 3 4 | 1 2 3 4

mp

5

9

p

How many phrases are in DAY 5? ____
Draw a whole rest.
I know my bass notes. How about you? Write the letter names in the stars on page 44.
Draw a half rest.
THE END!

13

mf

17

p

21

mf

f

1
5

DAY 1: I Am the King

______ **5-Finger Scale**

DON'T PRACTICE THIS!

See the king about the missing bar lines!

mf
Once up - on a time there lived a King.
f
I am the King. I am the King.

He would strut and ver - y loud - ly sing, "I am the King! I am the King!"
mf
f

Hark! The royal piano awaits my fingers.
But alas, the music has no **bar lines**. Put them in at ONCE!
Where's Buddy Barline when we need him?
Where's my pencil?
DRAW BAR LINES TO HELP LITTLE TREBLE AND LITTLE BASS.

I find 3rds to be simply divine.
Put a ✓ over each measure with a 3rd.
EVERY measure has a 3rd!
No, Little Bass. Not all of them!
WHO IS RIGHT, LITTLE TREBLE OR LITTLE BASS? (circle one)

DON'T PRACTICE THIS!

DAY 2: I Am the King

______ 5-Finger Scale

1

Once up - on a time, there lived a Queen, lived a Queen, lived a Queen.

mf *f*

1
5

5

When the Queen was hap - py, she would sing, "I'm the Queen! I'm the Queen!"

mf *f*

9

5
La, la, la, la, when the Queen was hap - py, she would sing.
p
f
1

Hey, don't step on my robe!
Your Highness, I know how you love 3rds.
Yes, I adore them. Which DAY would be my favorite? (circle one)
DAY 3
DAY 4

DAY 3: I Am the King

DON'T PRACTICE THIS!

______ 5-Finger Scale

1
mf
First the Queen sang, "Ta ti - ti ta - ah, ta ti - ti ta - ah, ti - ti - ti - ti ta - ah."

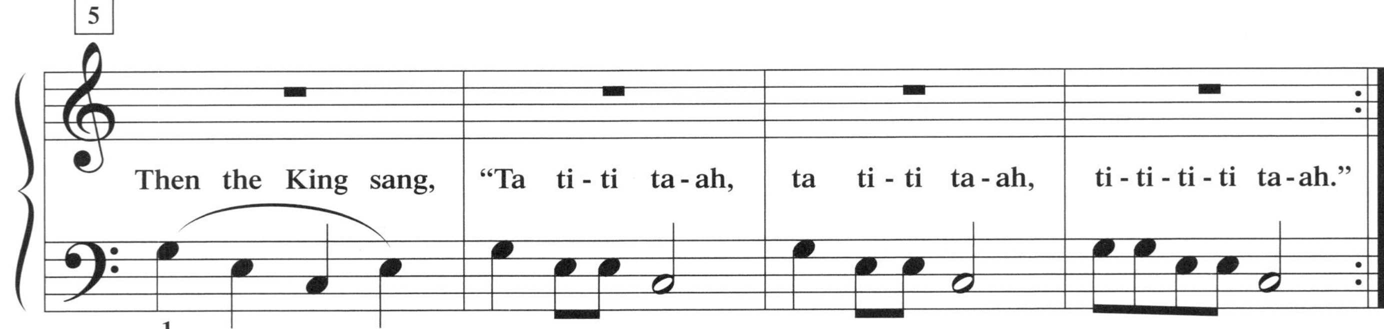
5
Then the King sang, "Ta ti - ti ta - ah, ta ti - ti ta - ah, ti - ti - ti - ti ta - ah."
1

DAY 4: I Am the King

______ 5-Finger Scale

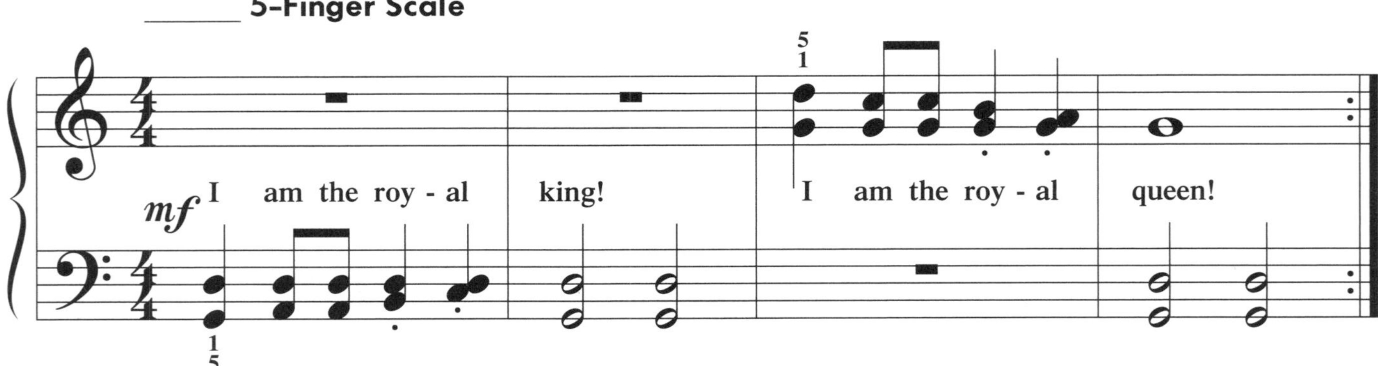
5
1
mf
I am the roy - al king! I am the roy - al queen!
1
5

DAY 5: I Am the King

______ 5-Finger Scale

DON'T PRACTICE THIS!

3rd
1
mf
"Knock, knock!" said the Queen.
"Who's there?" said the King.
1
3
"Wa - ter," said the Queen.
"Wa - ter who?" said the King.
5
"Wa - ter you do - ing
rit.
on my throne?" said the Queen.
Where's MY throne?
Great work, Sightreader!
Name the intervals in the crowns.

DAY 1: Our Detective Agency

DON'T
PRACTICE
THIS!

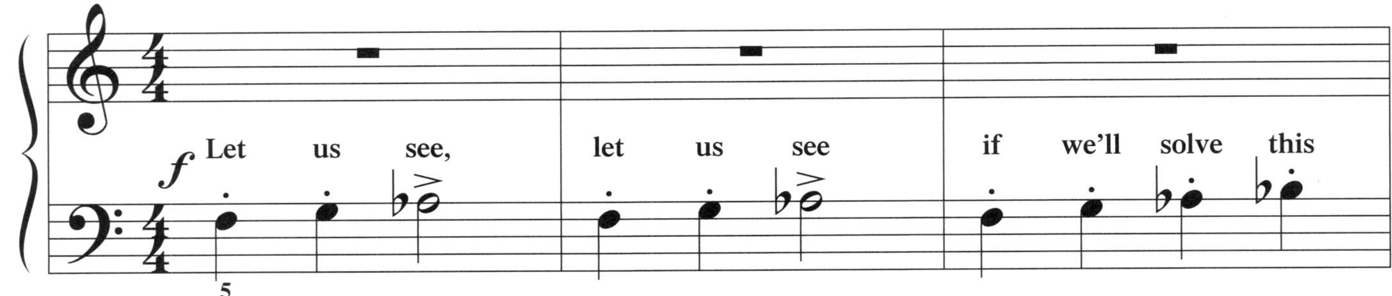
f
Let us see, let us see if we'll solve this
5

4
1
mys - ter - y.
p
Find all the clues to solve it.

7

f

We'll solve this mys - ter - y.

2

Something's fishy with this rhythm.
Put an X through each **incorrect measure**!

"SCAN EACH RHYTHM CARE-FUL-LY.
YOU MUST SOLVE THE MYS-TER-Y!"

RHYTHM ROAD

Another fishy rhythm! Put an X through the incorrect measures.
RHYTHM ROAD

DAY 2: Our Detective Agency

DON'T PRACTICE THIS!

1
Was - n't it odd? Was - n't it strange how the brief - case went
p
3

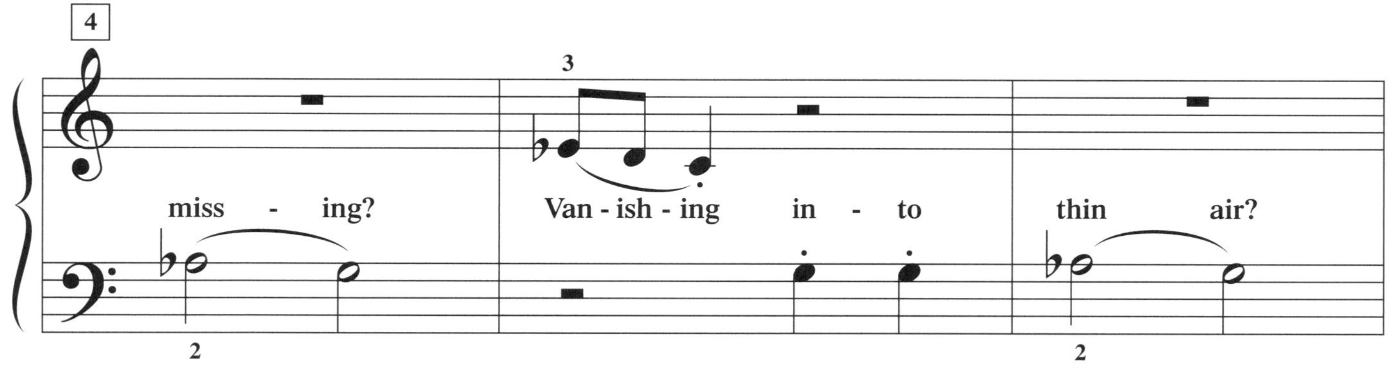
4
3
miss - ing? Van - ish - ing in - to thin air?
2
2

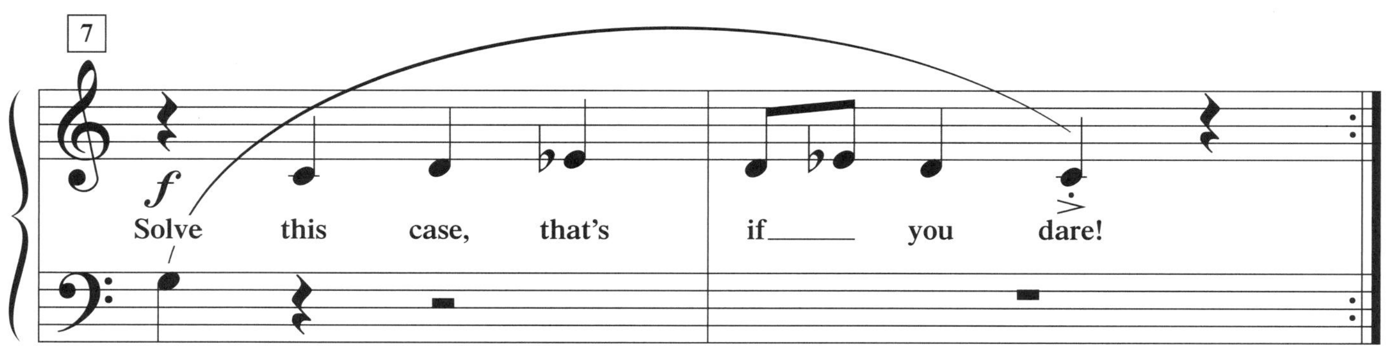
7
f
Solve this case, that's if you dare!

Gb
Bb
Bb
Eb
Eb
X out three **incorrect flats** above!
"SNOOP FOR FLATS THAT ARE NOT RIGHT. X THEM, GET THEM OUT OF SIGHT!"

DAY 3: Our Detective Agency

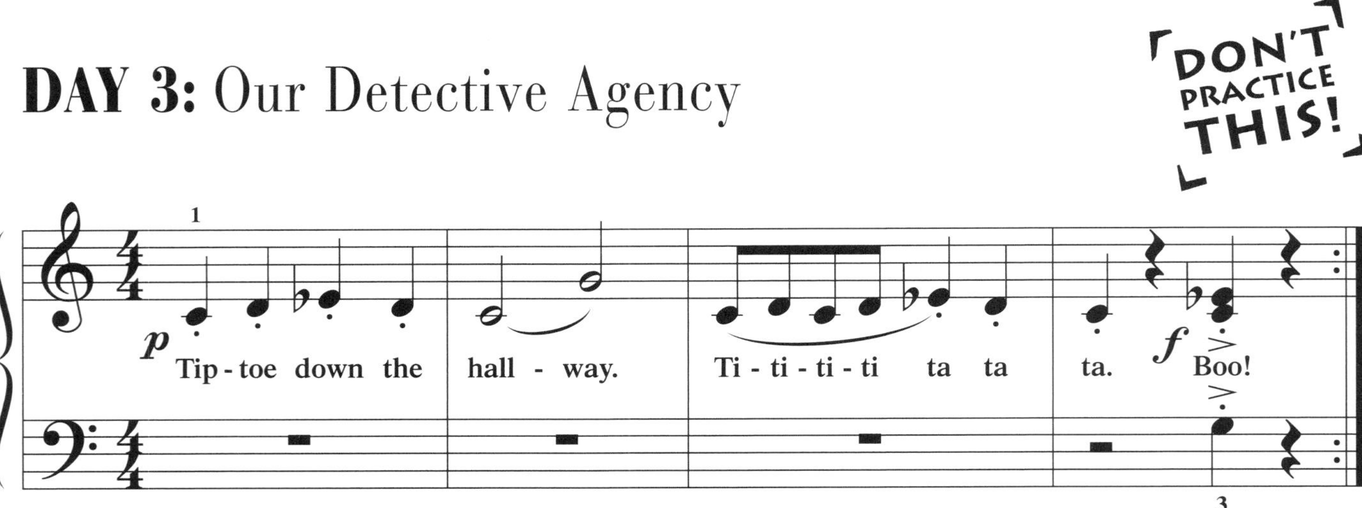
DON'T PRACTICE THIS!
1
p
Tip - toe down the hall - way. Ti - ti - ti - ti ta ta ta. Boo!
f
3

DAY 4: Our Detective Agency

1
2
p
Let's ex - plore, let's go snoop, let's go find some clues right now!
f
3

DAY 5: Our Detective Agency

DON'T PRACTICE THIS!
mf
Come to us to solve a mys - ter - y. We take cas - es
of com - plex - i - ty. Miss - ing dog, miss - ing hog, miss - ing mu - sic book.
We're the ex - pert sleuths to tell you where to look!

You made it to DAY 5. Great work from all of us music detectives!

No one will recognize us in these disguises.

DAY 1: This Old Man

______ 5-Finger Scale

DON'T
PRACTICE
THIS!

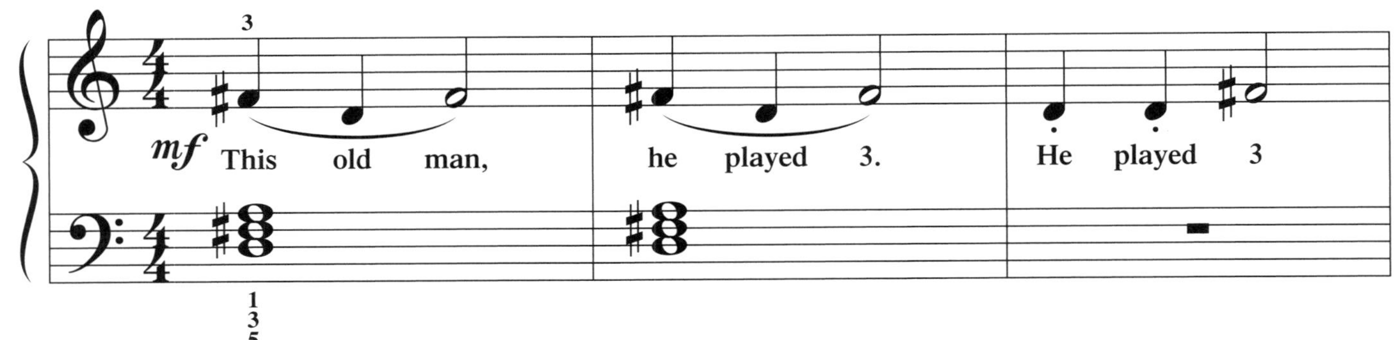

mf
This old man,
he played 3.
He played 3

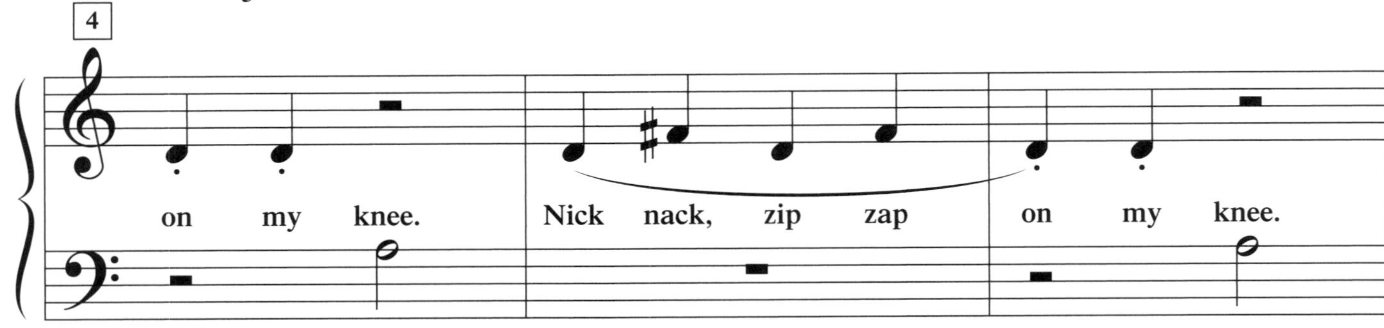

4
on my knee.
Nick nack, zip zap
on my knee.

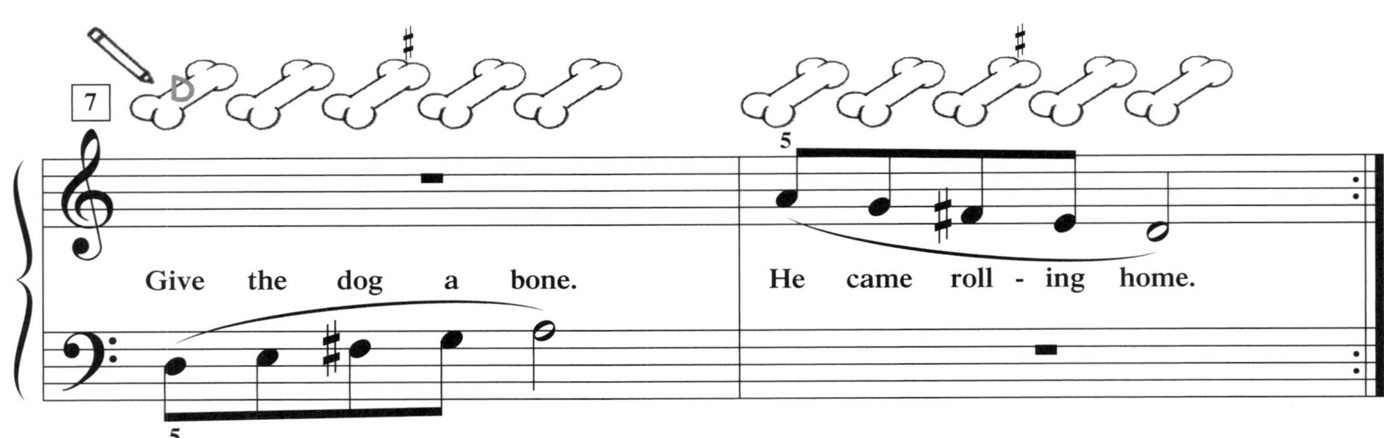

D
7
Give the dog a bone.
He came roll - ing home.

Write the **note name** from the D scale in each bone above!

Hello, young fella. Can you answer some **musical questions** for me?
Sure I can!
Bone, bone!

1. WHAT SCALE DOES DAY 2 USE? ____________
2. DOES EACH MEASURE STEP OR SKIP? (circle one)
3. WHAT SHARP IS USED IN EVERY MEASURE? ______ #

DAY 2: This Old Man

______ **5-Finger Scale**

DON'T PRACTICE THIS!

2nds or 3rds
2nds or 3rds
2nds or 3rds
2nds or 3rds
This old man,
he played 1.
He played nick nack
on my drum.
mf
5

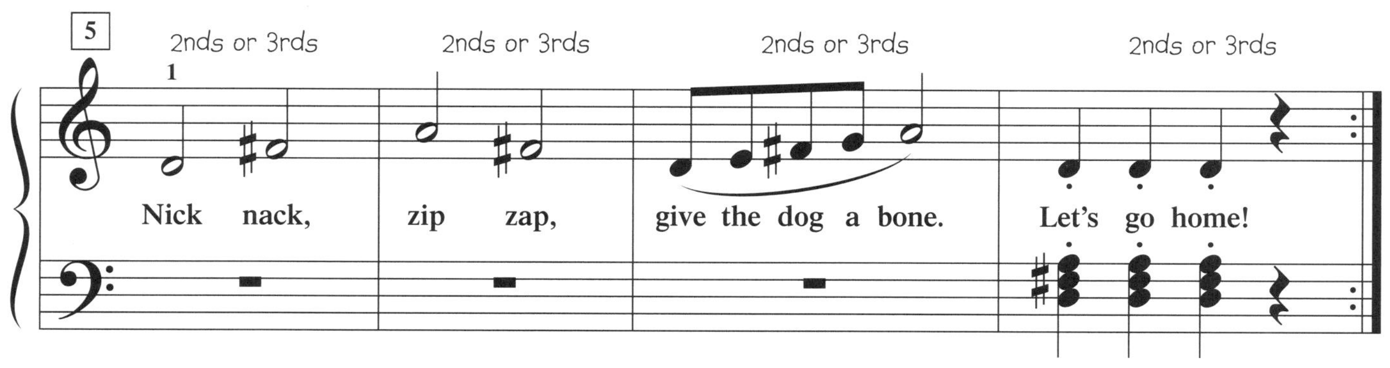

5
2nds or 3rds
2nds or 3rds
2nds or 3rds
2nds or 3rds
1
Nick nack,
zip zap,
give the dog a bone.
Let's go home!

DAY 3: This Old Man

DON'T
PRACTICE
THIS!

_____ 5-Finger Scale

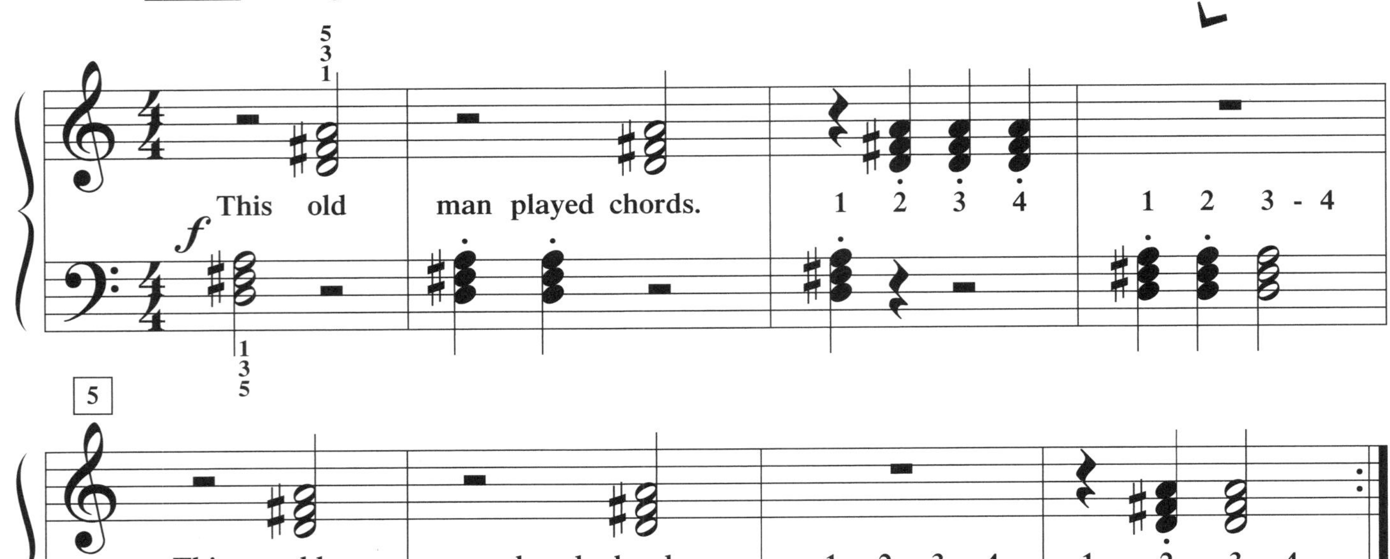
5
3
1
This old
man played chords.
1 2 3 4
1 2 3 - 4
f
1
3
5

5
This old
man loved chords.
1 - 2 - 3 - 4
1 2 3 - 4
p
f

DAY 4: This Old Man

_____ 5-Finger Scale

1
This old man sang
ti - ti - ti - ti ta - ah.
This old man sang
ti - ti - ti - ti ta - ah.
mf
1
Wow!
This old man rocks!
Yahoo!
Which day has
staccato notes?
DAY 3 or DAY 4?
(circle)

DAY 5
You're doing GREAT, sightreader!
Whew...just made it. Now write the **letter names** in each shoe below.
Ruff!

DAY 5: This Old Man

_____ 5-Finger Scale

DON'T PRACTICE THIS!

This old man came roll - ing home. This old man came roll - ing home.

Roll - ing home, roll - ing home, roll - ing home, roll - ing home.

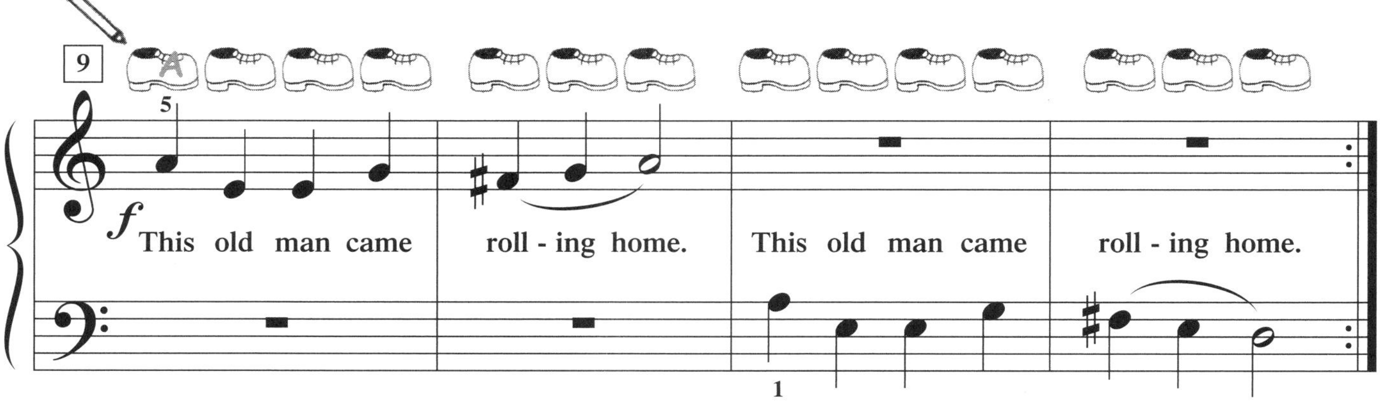
A
This old man came roll - ing home. This old man came roll - ing home.

DAY 1: Spring

______ 5-Finger Scale

DON'T PRACTICE THIS!

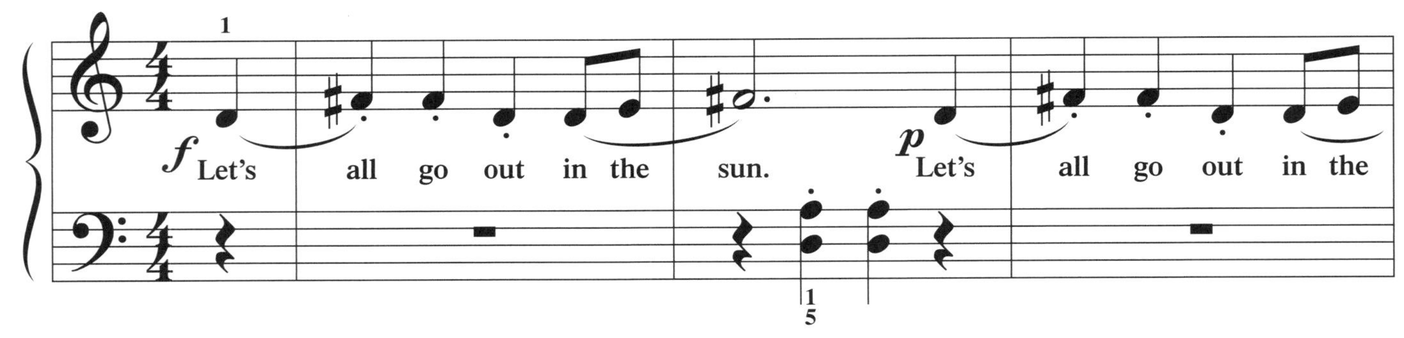
1
f Let's all go out in the sun.
p Let's all go out in the
1
5

4
sun.
f Let's sing and play.
p Let's sing and play.

WHO IS RIGHT? (circle one)
"Spell" the D major chord!
Hooray! Mr. Vivaldi is teaching today!
Spring has sprung!
D-F♯-A
D-E-F♯
VIVALDI

Which 3 flowers have a **half rest**?
Circle those flowers!

DAY 2: Spring

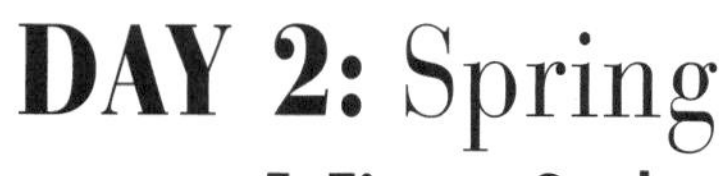
5-Finger Scale

DON'T PRACTICE THIS!

1
Let's walk in the bright sun - shine. (2 - 3) Let's
f
1 3

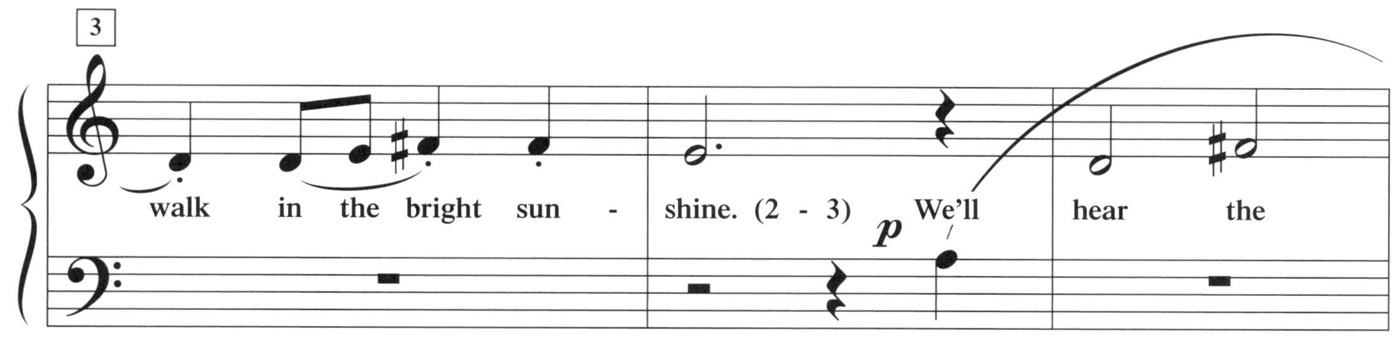
3
walk in the bright sun - shine. (2 - 3) We'll hear the
p

6
5
birds sing out in the bright sun - shine.
f

DAY 3: Spring

______ 5-Finger Scale

DON'T PRACTICE THIS!

Notice and feel the quarter rests.

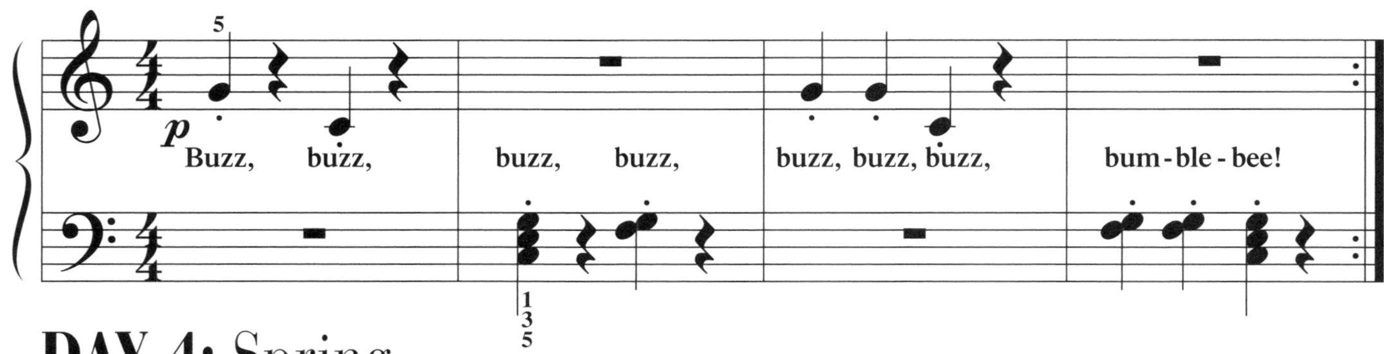
5
p
Buzz, buzz, buzz, buzz, buzz, buzz, buzz, bum-ble-bee!
1
3
5

DAY 4: Spring

______ 5-Finger Scale

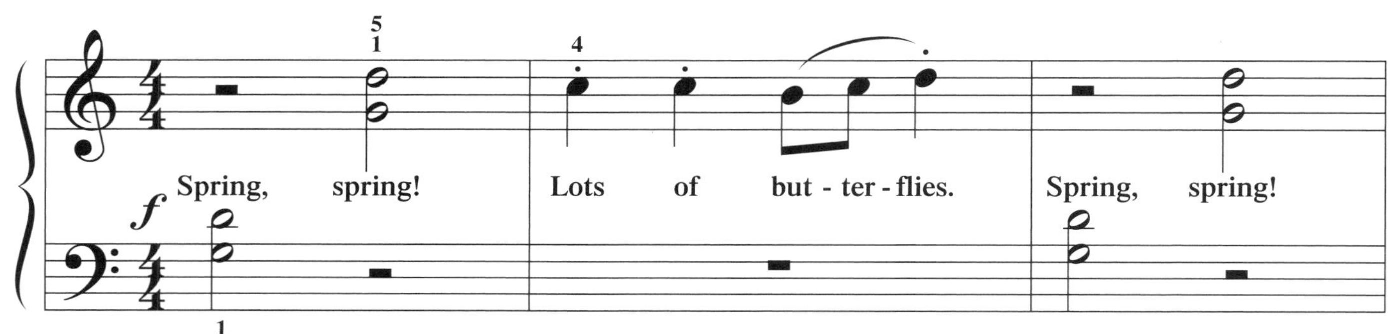
5
1
4
f
Spring, spring! Lots of but-ter-flies. Spring, spring!
1
5

4
Lots of but-ter-flies.
p
But-ter-fly in the sky!

Write 1234 for this rhythm.
Clap and count aloud!
RHYTHM ROAD
Ex. 1 2 3 4

Good to visit, Mr. Vivaldi!
Sightreader, can you write each **interval** in the butterfly?
DAY 5! Congratulations, sightreader, and good of you to join us, Mr. Bach!
BACH
VIVALDI

DAY 5: Spring

_____ 5-Finger Scale

DON'T PRACTICE THIS!

3rd

f The spring is here, spring is here,

5th

spring is here, spring is here. Flow - ers bloom,

p

flow - ers bloom, but - ter-flies, but - ter - flies here and there!

f

Ahoy, mateys!
If ye be needin' adventure, proceed!
Sightread and be quick about it!
ARRR!

DAY 1: Pirate of the North Sea
_____ 5-Finger Scale

DON'T PRACTICE THIS!

mf
Yo ho! Yo ho ho, pi-rates on the sea.

5
Yo ho! Treas - ures to find!

9
p
Yo ho ho! Yo ho ho! Treas - ures to find!
f

DAY 2: Pirate of the North Sea

_____ 5-Finger Scale

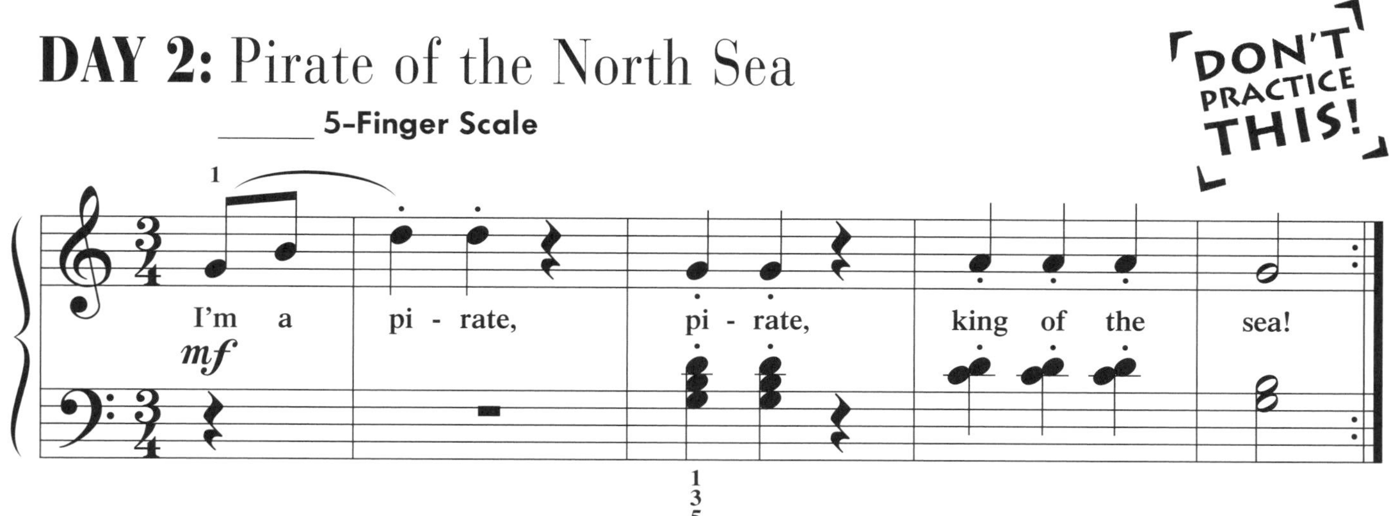
DON'T PRACTICE THIS!
I'm a pi - rate, pi - rate, king of the sea!
mf

DAY 3: Pirate of the North Sea

_____ 5-Finger Scale

mf They call me the cap - tain, the king of the sea! I'm

5

search - ing for dia - monds and ru - bies__ for__ me!

Yo Ho!

Shiver me timbers!

Me hearties, sightread up a storm. Then write the **note names** in the doubloons above.

Aye, Aye.

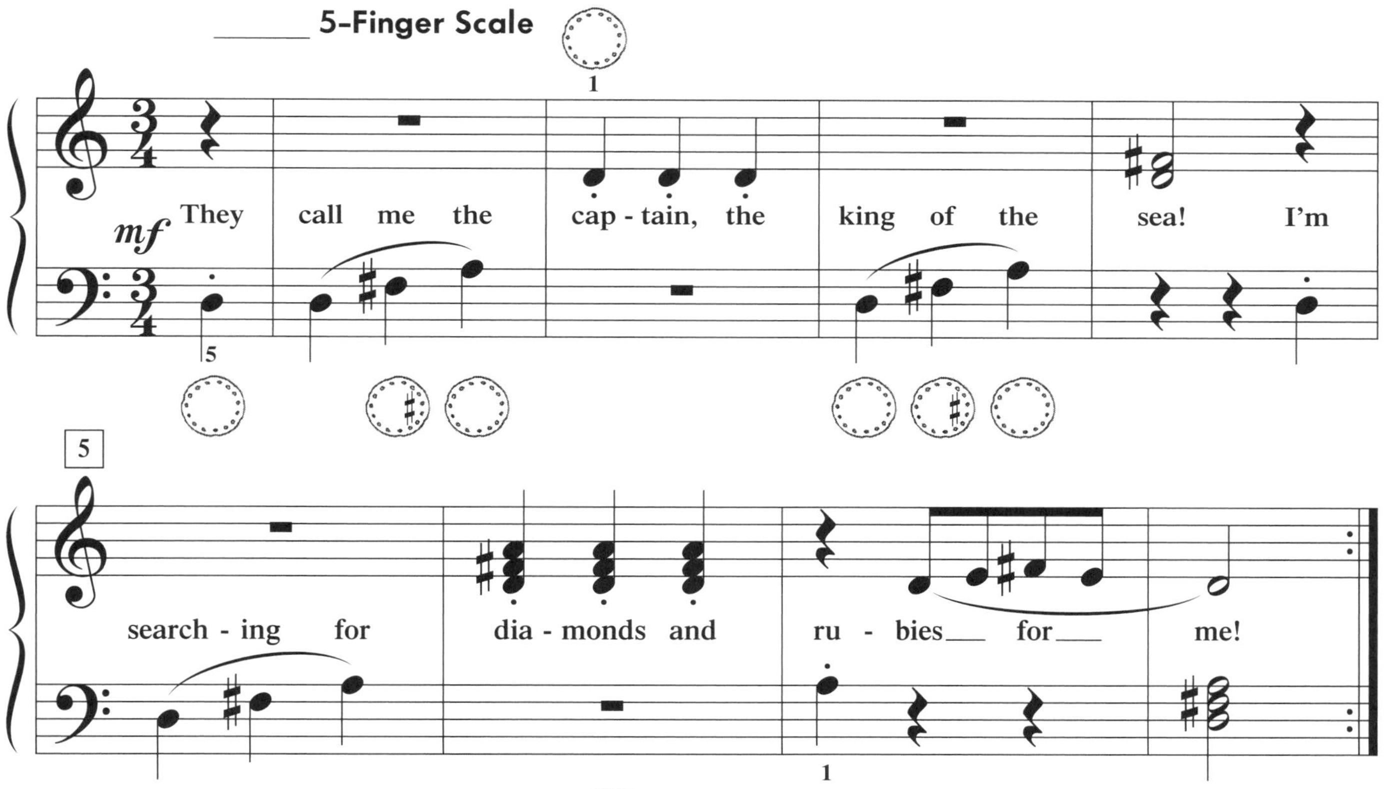

DON'T
PRACTICE
THIS!

DAY 4: Pirate of the North Sea

_____ 5-Finger Scale

mf
There's a pi - rate that's danc - ing, pi - rate that's danc - ing,

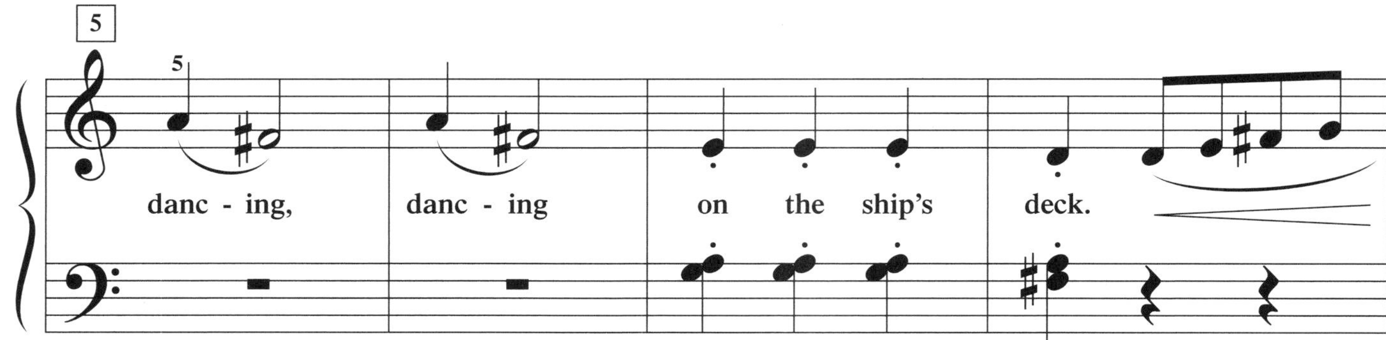
5
danc - ing, danc - ing on the ship's deck.

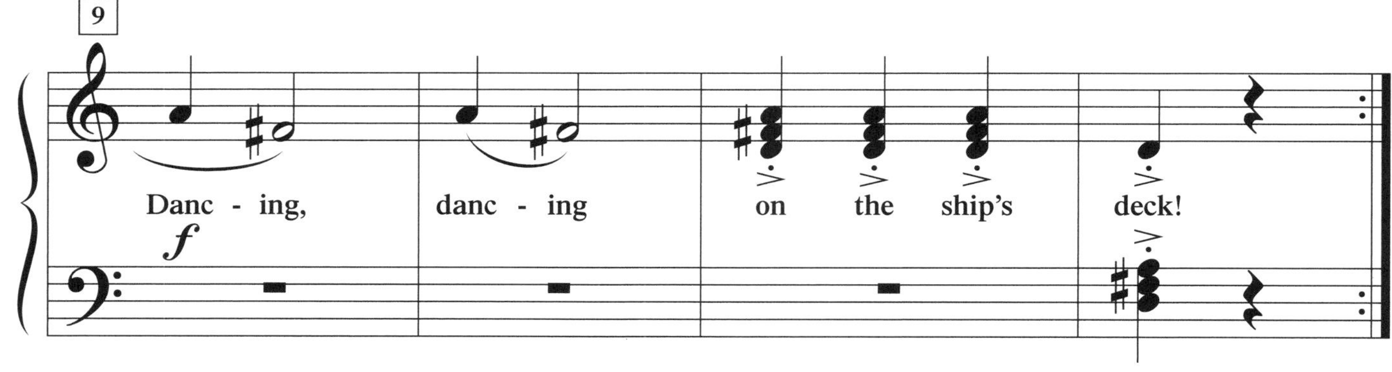
9
Danc - ing, danc - ing on the ship's deck!
f

Me hearties, on what beat does this sea song begin?
Beat 3.
Beat 1.
WHO IS RIGHT? (circle)

Ahoy!
'Til next time.
ARRR!
Good work!
DAY 5! Congratulations, brave sightreader.
Meet me rugged crew.

DAY 5: Pirate of the North Sea

_____ 5-Finger Scale

DON'T PRACTICE THIS!

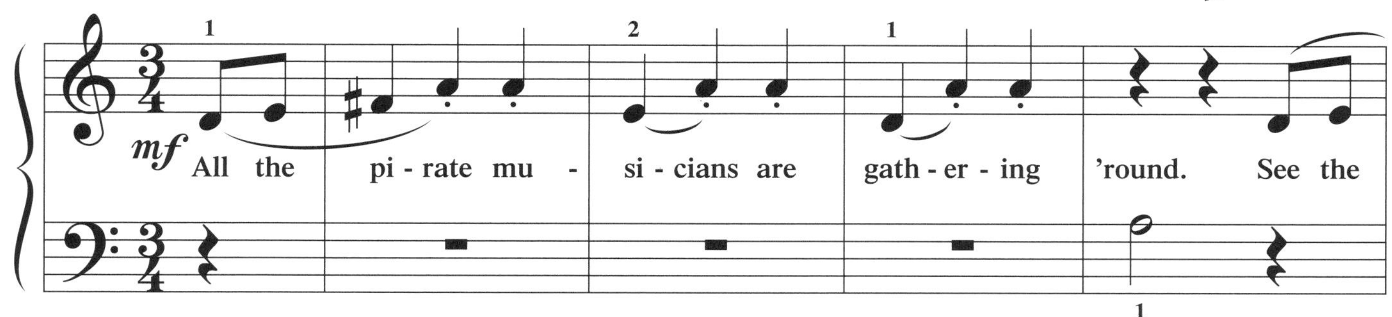
mf
All the pi - rate mu - si - cians are gath - er - ing 'round. See the

5
tin cans and whis - tles and fid - dles mak - ing the sound. And their
f

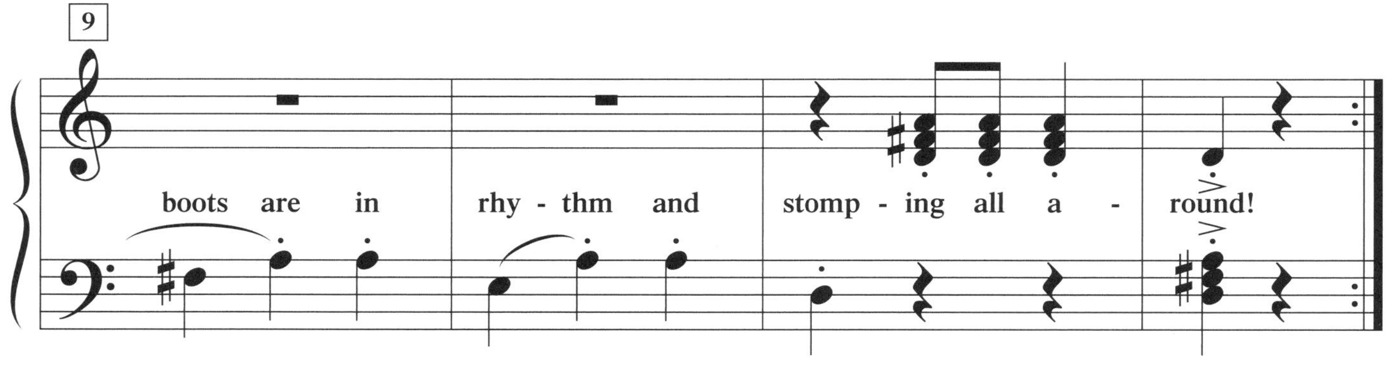
9
boots are in rhy - thm and stomp - ing all a - round!

Hello from up high! Write the **note names** in the stars below.

It's a bird, it's a plane, it's Peter Pan!

DAY 1: Peter Pan's Flight

______ **5-Finger Scale**

DON'T PRACTICE THIS!

f A

Star - ry night, *p* star - ry night,

5

mf Pe - ter Pan flies on a star - ry night.

DAY 2: Peter Pan's Flight

_____ 5-Finger Scale

DON'T PRACTICE THIS!
Ti - ti - ti - ti ta.
Star - ry night!
Star - ry night!
Pe - ter Pan flies in the night.
Pe - ter Pan flies in the night.
Hop aboard, little friends!
How many measures use a broken A chord?
3 measures.
4 measures.
WHO IS RIGHT? (circle)

DON'T PRACTICE THIS!

DAY 3: Peter Pan's Flight

______ 5-Finger Scale

f Ta, ta, ta ti - ti ta, ta ti - ti ta.

(prepare L.H.)

5

p Ta, ta, ta ti - ti ta, ta ti - ti ta.

DAY 4: Peter Pan's Flight

______ 5-Finger Scale

See Peter Pan about the missing bar lines!

Pe - ter Pan is tak - ing flight on this star - ry, star - ry night.

f-*p* *on repeat*

Hey, sightreader! Before we fly, draw **bar lines** after every **3 beats** for DAY 4.
Really, really, really high!
Take us for a ride!
We want to fly!

Congratulations! You're taking off with sightreading!
How many measures use the interval of a 3rd?
5 measures.
3 measures.
2 measures.
4 measures.
WHO IS RIGHT? (circle one)

DAY 5: Peter Pan's Flight

DON'T PRACTICE THIS!

_____ 5-Finger Scale

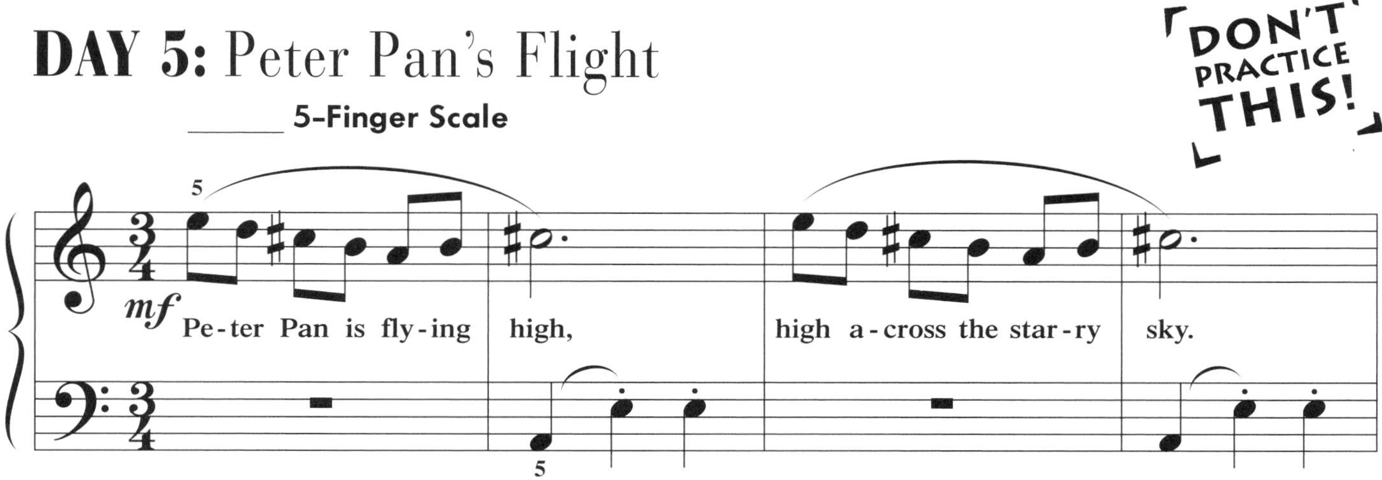
5
mf
Pe-ter Pan is fly-ing high, high a-cross the star-ry sky.
5

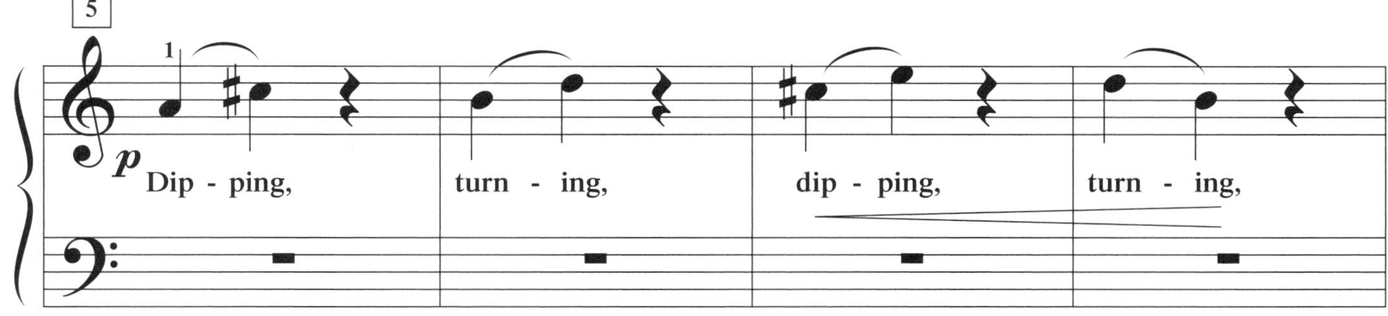
5
1
p
Dip - ping, turn - ing, dip - ping, turn - ing,

9
mf
1
Pe-ter Pan is fly-ing high, high a-cross the star-ry sky.

DAY 1: Aardvark Boogie
_____ 5-Finger Scale

DON'T PRACTICE THIS!

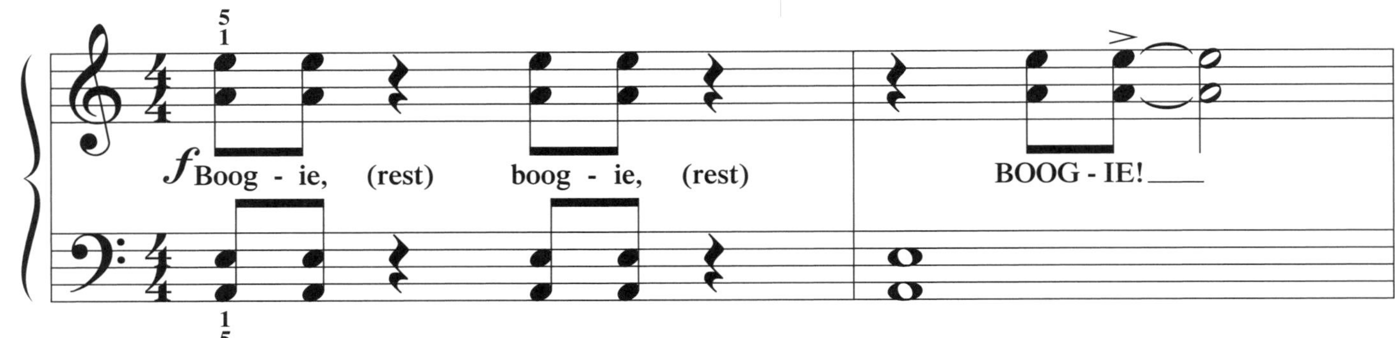
f Boog - ie, (rest) boog - ie, (rest)
BOOG - IE!

3

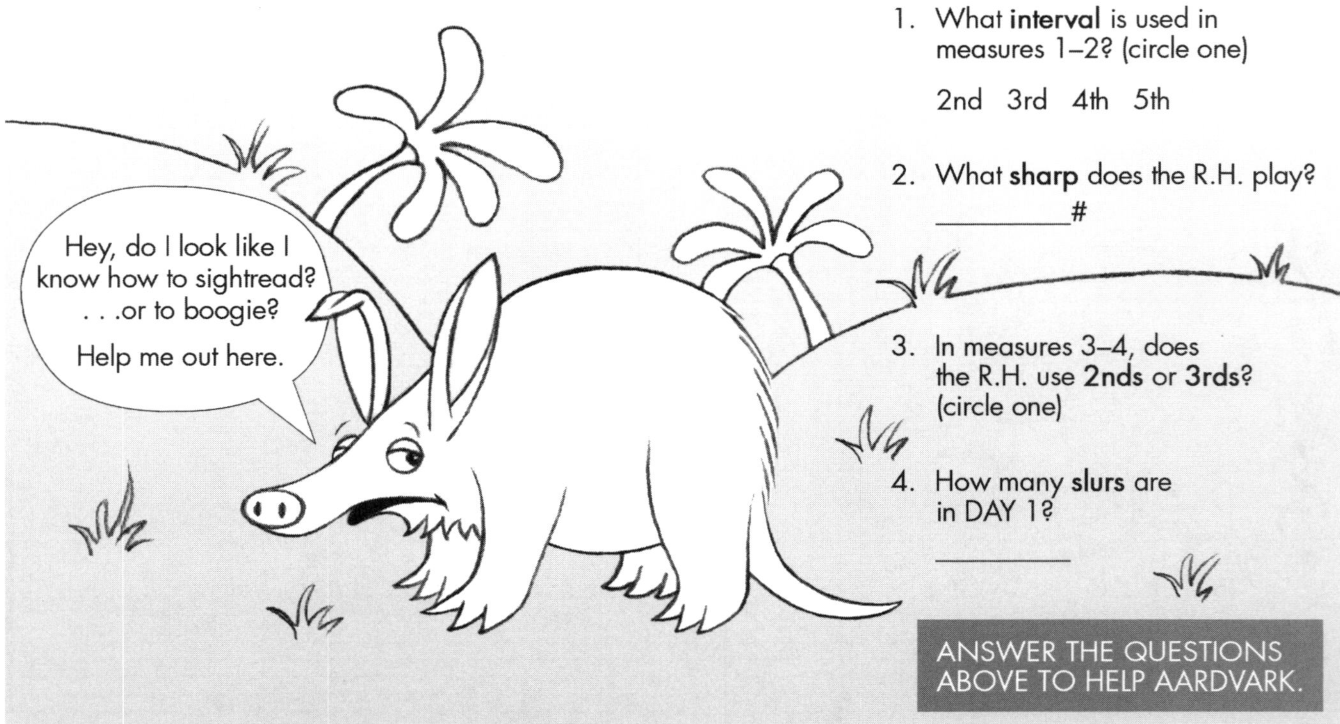
Hey, do I look like I know how to sightread? . . .or to boogie?
Help me out here.

1. What **interval** is used in measures 1–2? (circle one)

   2nd 3rd 4th 5th

2. What **sharp** does the R.H. play?

   _________#

3. In measures 3–4, does the R.H. use **2nds** or **3rds**? (circle one)

4. How many **slurs** are in DAY 1?

   ____

ANSWER THE QUESTIONS ABOVE TO HELP AARDVARK.

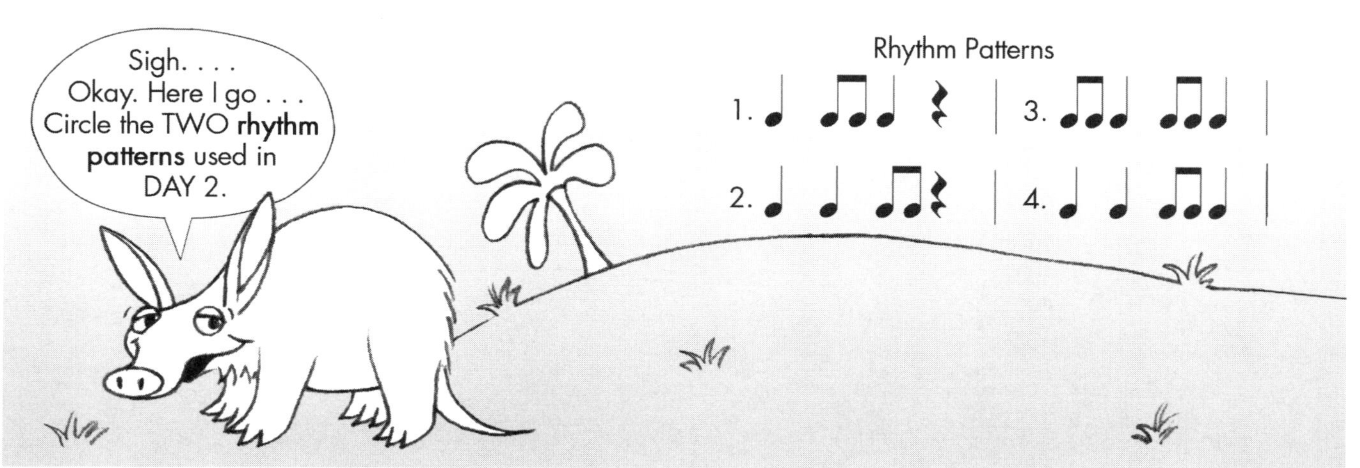
Sigh. . . .
Okay. Here I go . . .
Circle the TWO **rhythm patterns** used in DAY 2.
Rhythm Patterns
1.
2.
3.
4.

DAY 2: Aardvark Boogie

_____ 5-Finger Scale

DON'T PRACTICE THIS!

mf

Ta ti - ti ta, (rest) Ta ta ti - ti ta.

1
5

4

1
4

7

This one is really, really tricky. Chord Guy had to tell me the answer… In DAY 3, which measure uses a **half step**? (circle one)
MEASURE 1
MEASURE 3
MEASURE 2
MEASURE 4
* Answer at the bottom.

DAY 3: Aardvark Boogie

_____ **5-Finger Scale**

DON'T PRACTICE THIS!

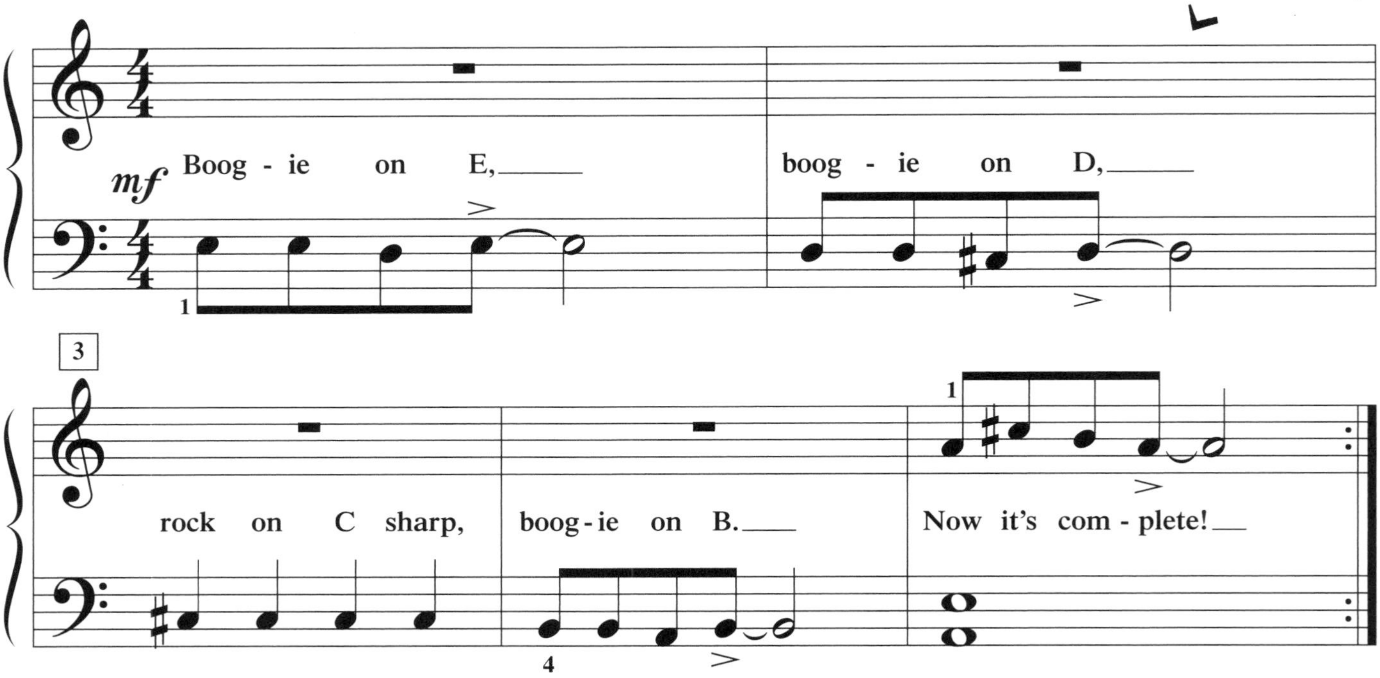

mf Boog - ie on E,___ boog - ie on D,___

3

rock on C sharp, boog-ie on B.___ Now it's com - plete!___

DAY 4: Aardvark Boogie

_____ **5-Finger Scale**

f
Count: 1 + 2 3 4
p

Answer: measure 2 (D to C#).

DAY 5: Aardvark Boogie
DON'T PRACTICE THIS!
_____ 5-Finger Scale
Thanks, Aardvark. Bye.
Bye for now.
Well, congratulations. I'm gonna go now . . . gonna go eat some ants.
Maybe I'll see you again . . . Bye.

DAY 1: Whirling Leaves

______ 5-Finger Scale

Hold the damper pedal down throughout.

DON'T PRACTICE THIS!

5th
1
5
mf
Whirl - ing leaves are swirl - ing a-round.
mp
5
2
4
Leaves are fall - ing down to the ground.
mf

7
mp
Whirl-ing leaves, whirl-ing leaves fall.
mf
p

Write the intervals in the leaves above.
My Hat!
My dots are blowing away!

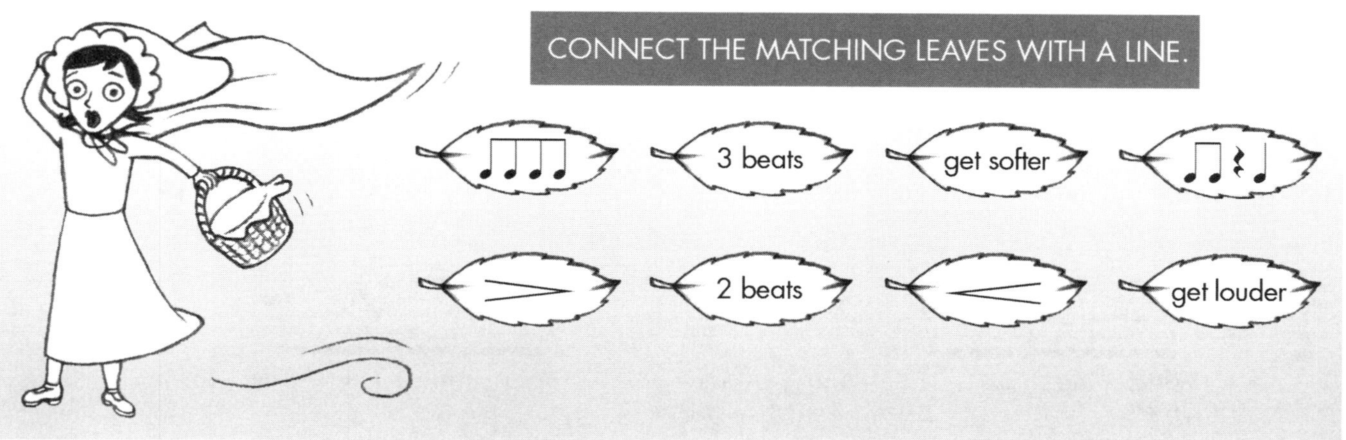
CONNECT THE MATCHING LEAVES WITH A LINE.
3 beats
get softer
2 beats
get louder

DAY 2: Whirling Leaves

DON'T PRACTICE THIS!

_____ 5-Finger Scale

Hold the damper pedal down throughout.

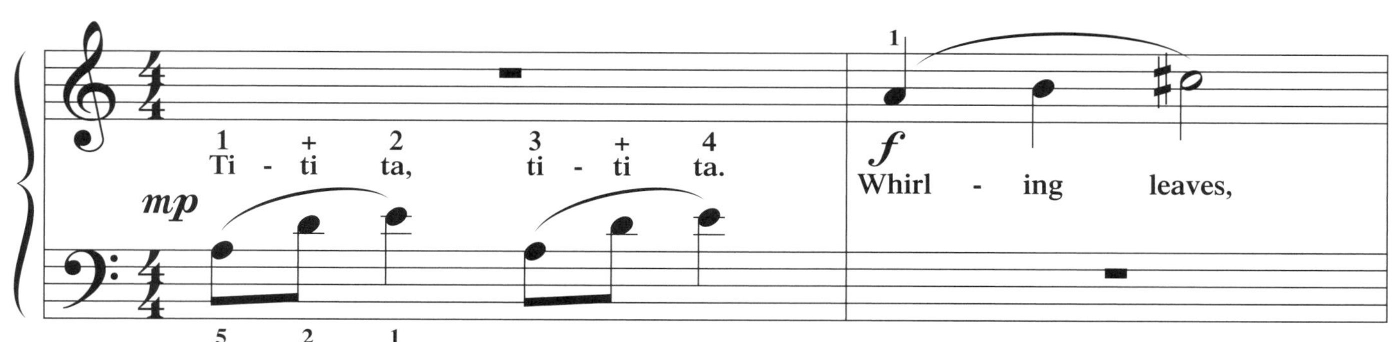
1 + 2 3 + 4
Ti - ti ta, ti - ti ta.
mp
f
Whirl - ing leaves,

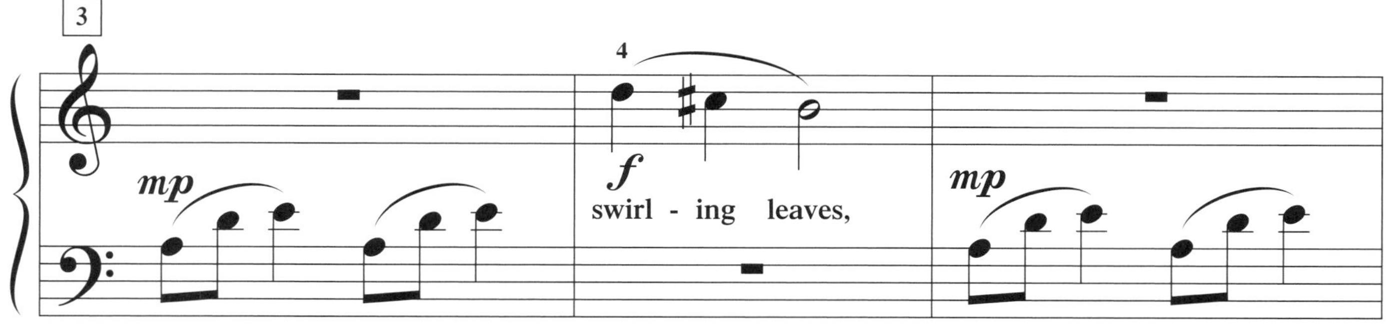
mp
f
swirl - ing leaves,
mp

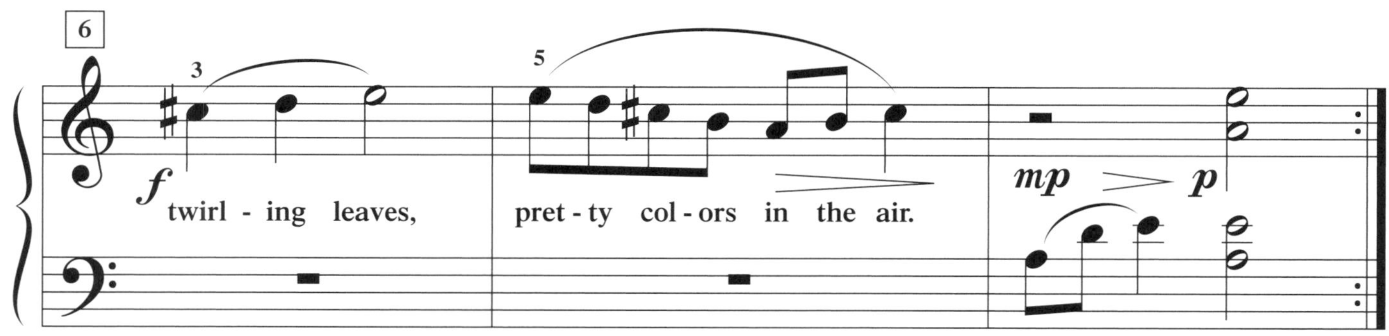
f
twirl - ing leaves,
pret - ty col - ors in the air.
mp p

DAY 3: Whirling Leaves

______ 5-Finger Scale

DON'T PRACTICE THIS!

Hold the damper pedal down throughout.

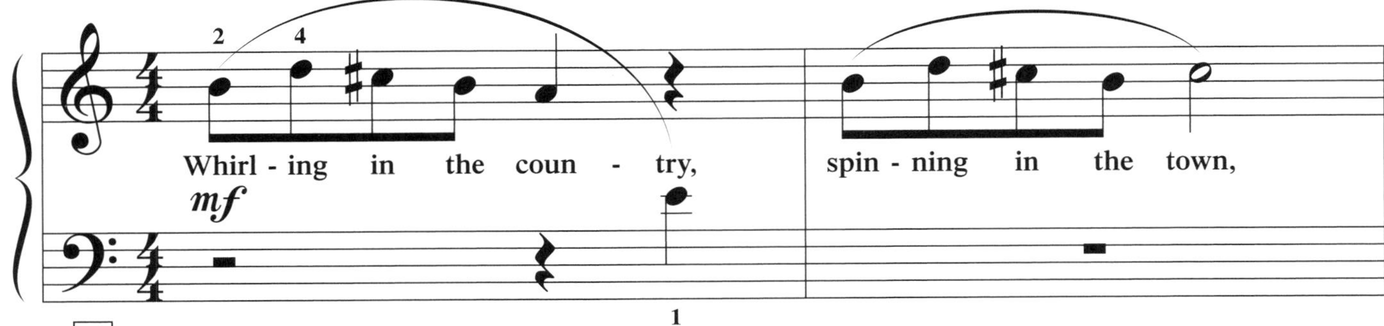

2
4
Whirl - ing in the coun - try,
spin - ning in the town,
mf
1

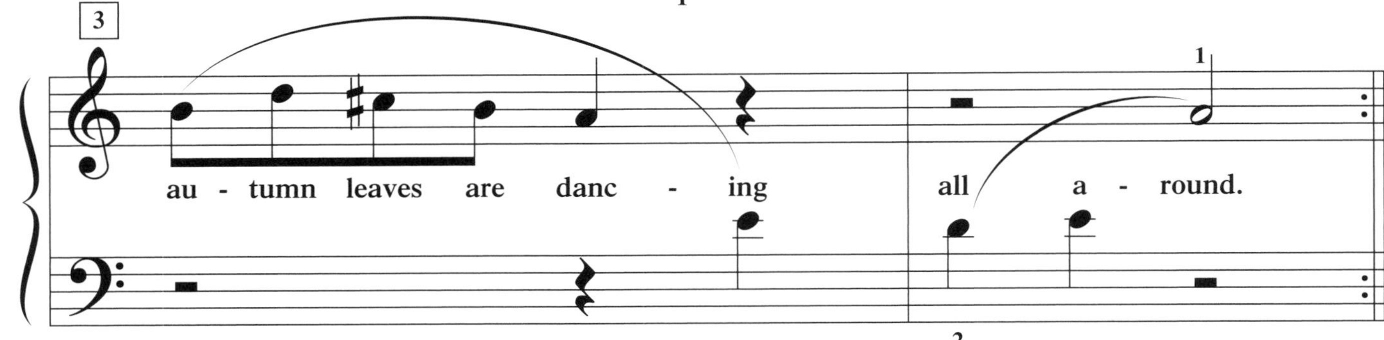

3
1
au - tumn leaves are danc - ing
all a - round.
2

DAY 4: Whirling Leaves

______ 5-Finger Scale

Without pedal.

1
Run-ning, run-ning, walk, walk,
run-ning, run-ning, walk, walk,
walk, walk, walk!
p
f
5

RHYTHM ROAD
Draw bar lines for this rhythm.

Congratulations! DAY 5!

DAY 5: Whirling Leaves

______ **5-Finger Scale**

DON'T PRACTICE THIS!

mf All the leaves are fall - ing. Let's go play!

3 Make a big leaf pile to - day!

f

6

p

Be careful with that sword!

The Great Swordsman requests the number of measures with this rhythm pattern: ♫ ♩ ♩

2 measures.

3 measures.

5 measures.

WHO IS RIGHT? (circle one)

DAY 1: Sword Dance

_____ **Major/minor 5-Finger Scale**

DON'T PRACTICE THIS!

Make way!
The swordsman!
(Run-ning, walk, walk)
How quickly he moves!

DAY 2: Sword Dance
______ Major/minor 5-Finger Scale
DON'T PRACTICE THIS!
He moves smoothly!
mp
f
5
On guard!
f
p
f
What musical symbol helps me to glide smoothly?
the slur
the crescendo
the... EEEK!
the staccatos
the rests
the accents
WHO IS RIGHT? (circle one)

D-F-G
D-F-A
Which 3 **letter names** are used for DAY 3 and 4?
The D minor scale?
D-E-F
Beats me!
WHO IS RIGHT? (circle one)

DAY 3: Sword Dance

______ **Major/minor 5-Finger Scale**

DON'T PRACTICE THIS!

How lightly he steps!
Count: 1 2 3 1 2 3 1 2 + 3
mp

DAY 4: Sword Dance

______ **Major/minor 5-Finger Scale**

f
p
5
He leaps and lands perfectly with his sword!
f

DAY 5: Sword Dance

_____ Major/minor 5-Finger Scale

DON'T PRACTICE THIS!
D
He dances and spins.
mf
Count: 1 + 2 + 3
1 2 3
He raises his sword.
f
He bows!
Let's get to the point. CONGRATULATIONS!
DAY 5! You did it!
Your mind is sharp!
Write the letter name in each hat.

DAY 1: In an Old Castle
_____ Major/minor 5-Finger Scale
DON'T PRACTICE THIS!
mp
f
5
f
9
mf
rit.
p
Are the notes in parallel or contrary motion?
I hear piano music from the old castle!
CIRCLE ONE

DAY 2: In an Old Castle

_____ **Major/minor 5-Finger Scale**

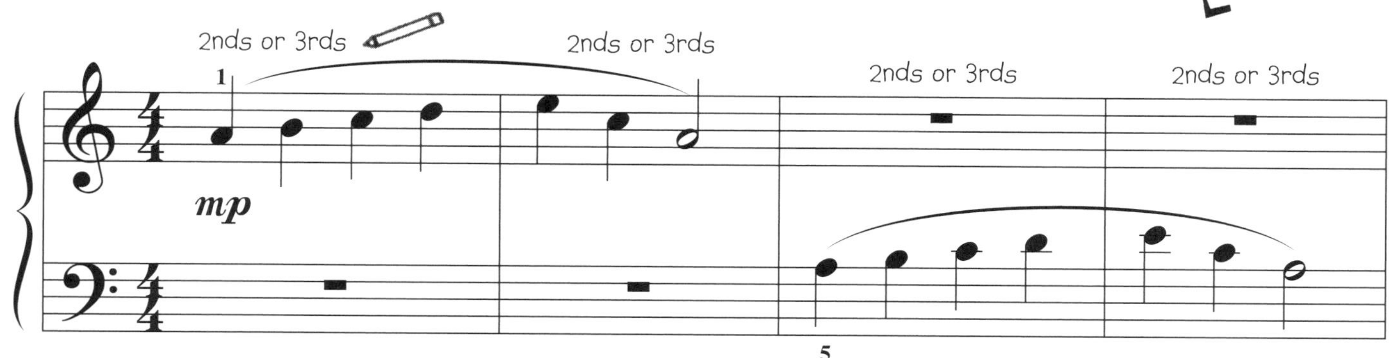

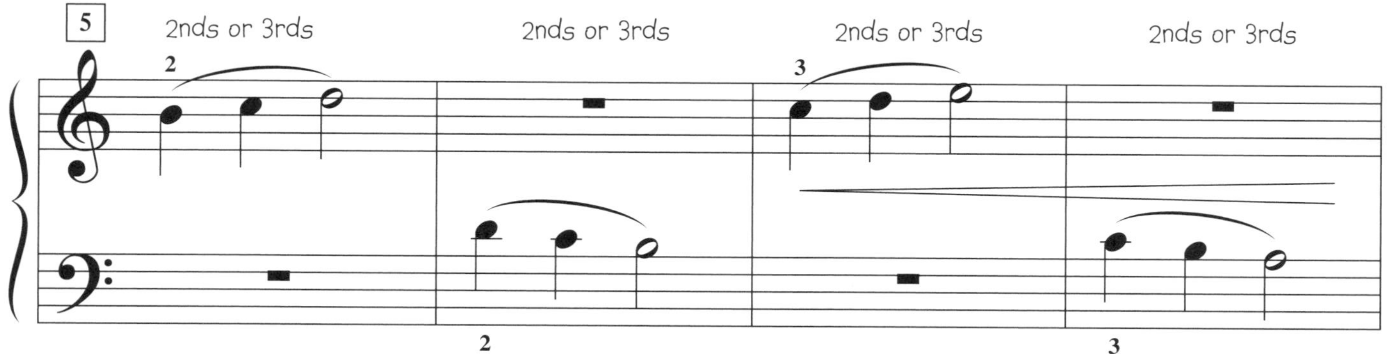

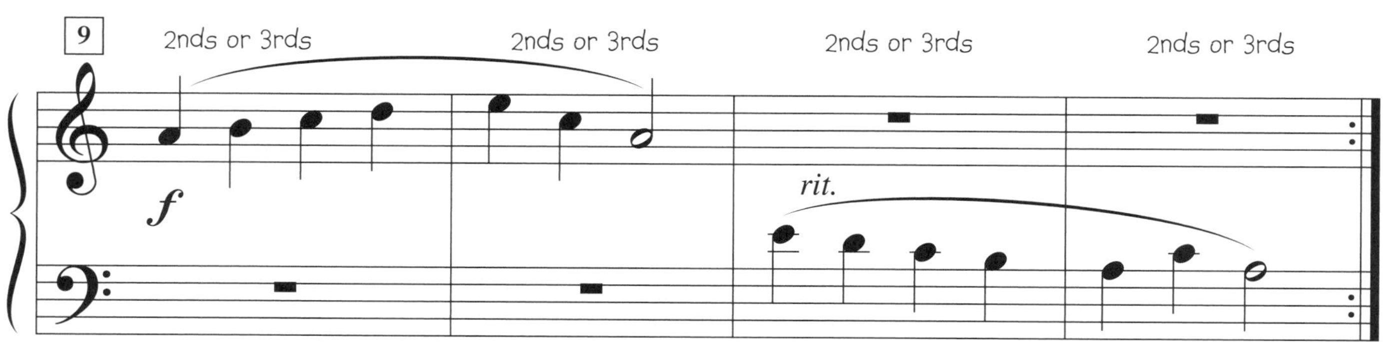

DAY 3: In an Old Castle

_____ Major/minor 5-Finger Scale

DON'T
PRACTICE
THIS!

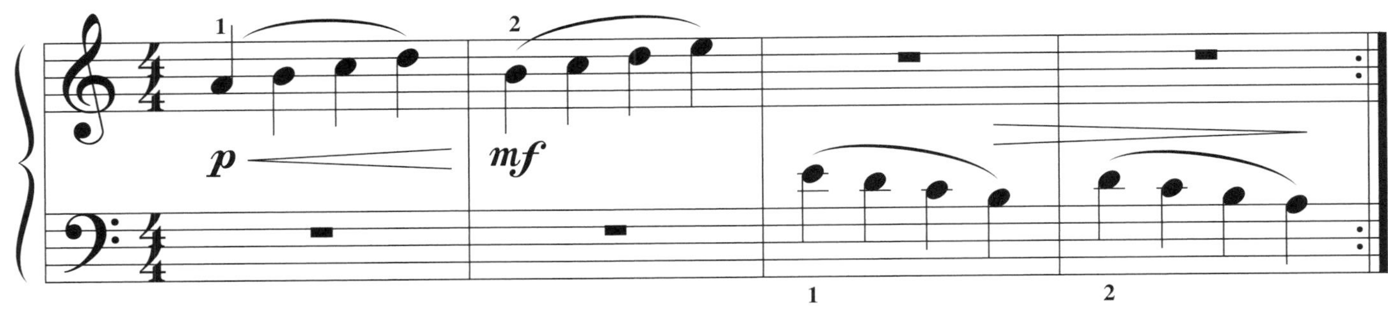
p
mf

DAY 4: In an Old Castle

_____ Major/minor 5-Finger Scale

mf

5

rit.

Which day has a **crescendo**? DAY 3 or DAY 4? (circle one)

Hurry up, aardvark. We're going in!

I'm a comin'...

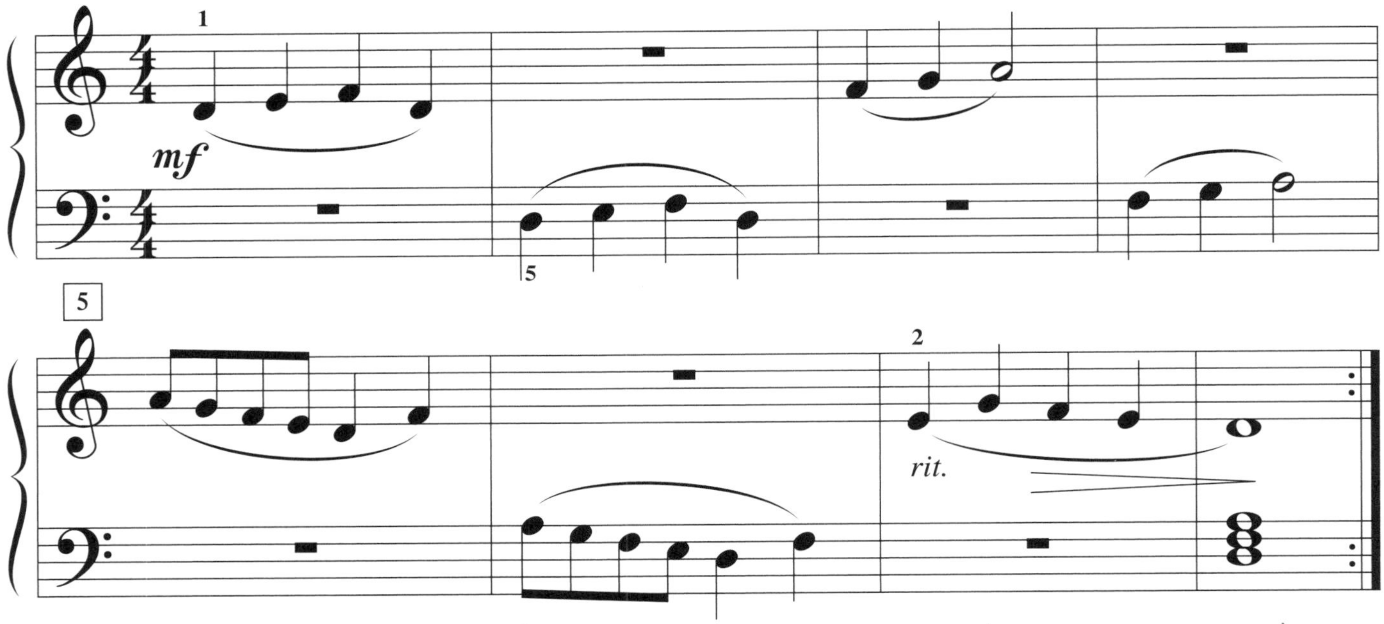

I hear music, too!
I'm a comin'...
Party at the castle!
SURPRISE!
...and GREAT WORK!
Write the note names in the flags.

DAY 5: In an Old Castle

____ Major/minor 5-Finger Scale

DON'T PRACTICE THIS!

A

1 5 mf

5

5

9

f

3

1

ARRR! What **5-finger scale** will ye be usin'? And if ye say major, you'll be walkin' the plank!
Keep it cool, man . . .
Scoobie doobie doo.
Chill, dude.
We're the razzamatazz!
Boop shoo ba.

DAY 1: Jazz Blast

DON'T PRACTICE THIS!

______ **Major/minor 5-Finger Scale**

3
f
1
5
5

DAY 2: Jazz Blast

______ Major/minor 5-Finger Scale

DON'T PRACTICE THIS!
C
f
5
1
5
3
9
p
f
Hey, Piano Man, take it from the top!
. . . and-a 1, and-a 2, and-a you know what to do!
My fingers just want to go wild!
Write the **note names** in each string bass above.

Write 1234 under the correct beats.
Then tap it with your toes!
RHYTHM ROAD

DAY 3: Jazz Blast

______ Major/minor 5-Finger Scale

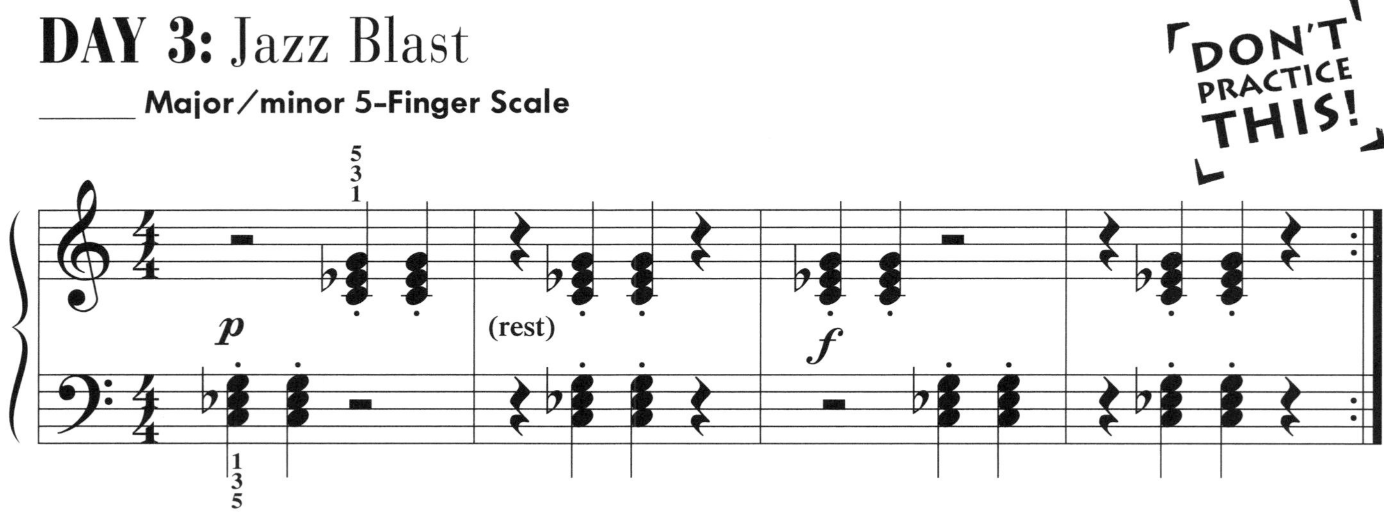
DON'T PRACTICE THIS!
p
(rest)
f

DAY 4: Jazz Blast

______ Major/minor 5-Finger Scale

Notice the L.H. position change in the last measure.

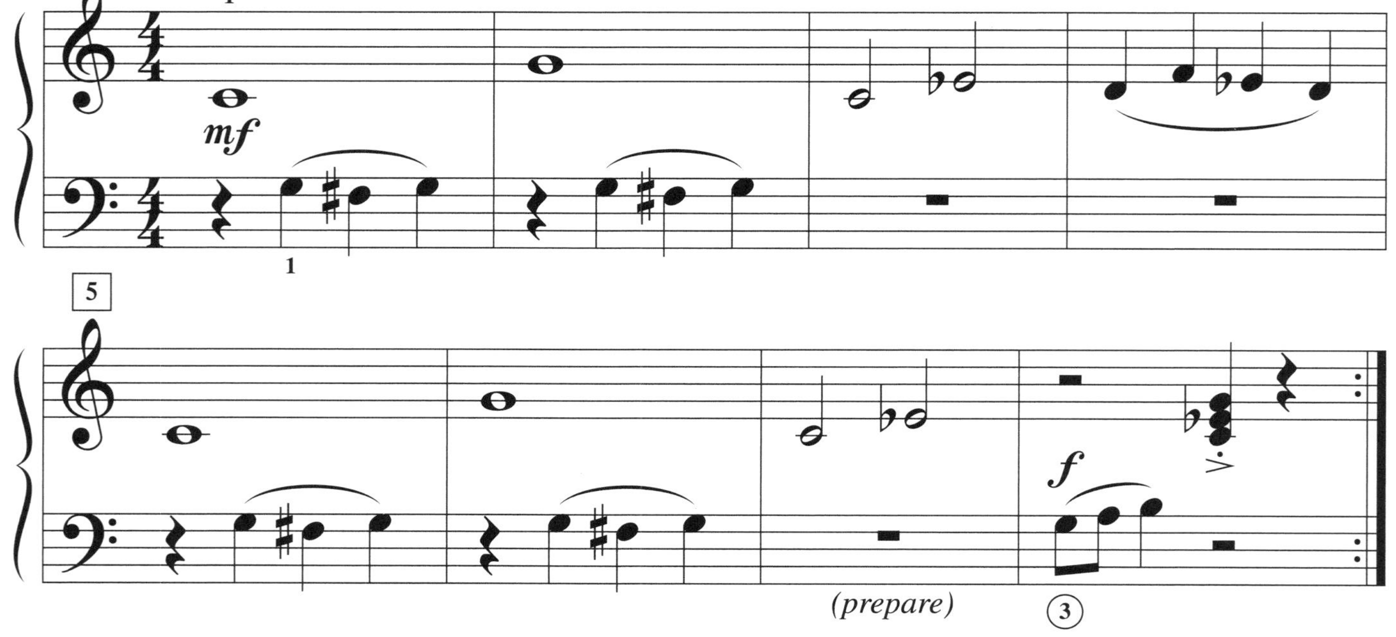
mf
f
(prepare)

DAY 5: Jazz Blast

______ Major/minor 5-Finger Scale

DON'T
PRACTICE
THIS!

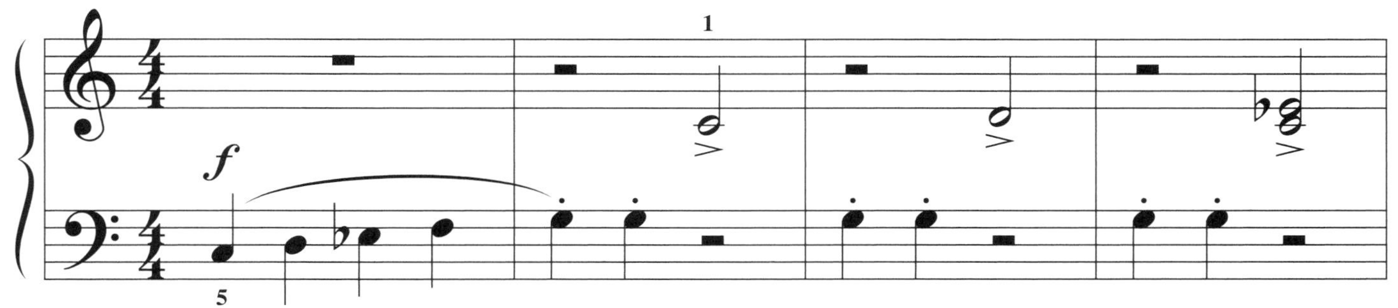
1
f
5

5
(rest)

9
mp
p
(1 - 2)
f

Sightreader, you're a CHAMPION! Only 6 pages to go. YAY!
I brought my friends.
Play on, Piano Man.
I'm layin' down the beat. Love it . . .

DAY 1: Snake Charmer

DON'T
PRACTICE
THIS!

_____ **Major/minor 5-Finger Scale**

Count: 1 2 + 3 4
p

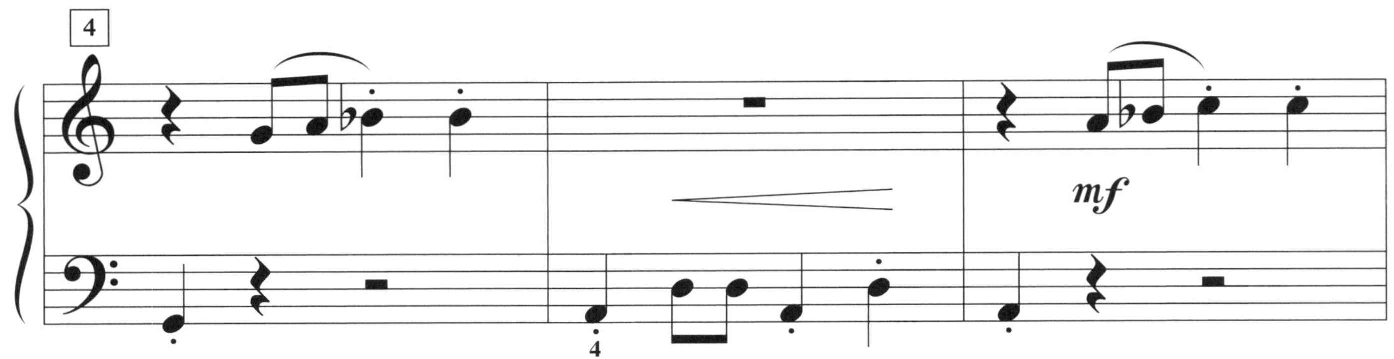
4
mf

7
f

I think she likes the aardvark!
Oh, dear . . .

WHAT INTERVAL IS USED THROUGHOUT DAY 2? (circle one)

2nd 3rd 4th 5th

She's moving in closer . . . let's call for backup!

Oh, oh dear . . .

DAY 2: Snake Charmer

DON'T PRACTICE THIS!

What do you do when a big snake likes you, and you're just a lit - tle
p
5

4
aard - vark? Yes, and you're just a lit - tle aard - vark?

It's working! She's playing the Brahms lullaby.
Go to sleep, snake-y.

DAY 3: Snake Charmer

DON'T PRACTICE THIS!

Nev-er fear, help is here.

We can charm her a-sleep.

Soon she'll be fast a-sleep.

See her eyes start to close.

DAY 4: Snake Charmer

DON'T PRACTICE THIS!
What will hap - pen now?
What will hap - pen now?
Will that snake fall fast a - sleep? Will she rest so still and deep? Sneak a - way, lit - tle aard - vark!
rit.
NAME THE NOTES IN THE VIOLINS ABOVE.
Hey, aardvark! You can't go to sleep, too. What do you think you're doin'?
Zzz . . .

CONGRATULATIONS!
BACH

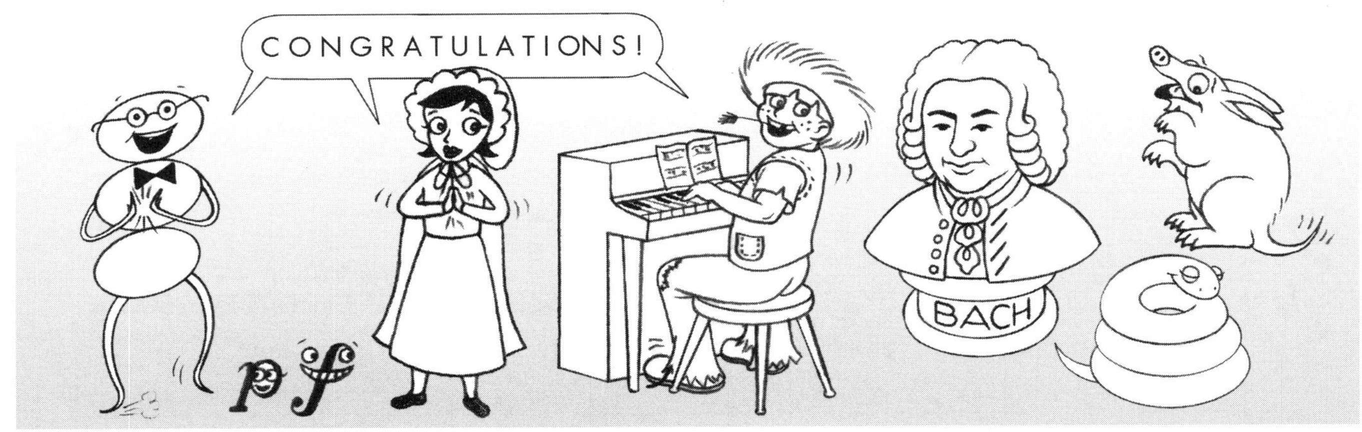

DAY 5: Snake Charmer

DON'T PRACTICE THIS!

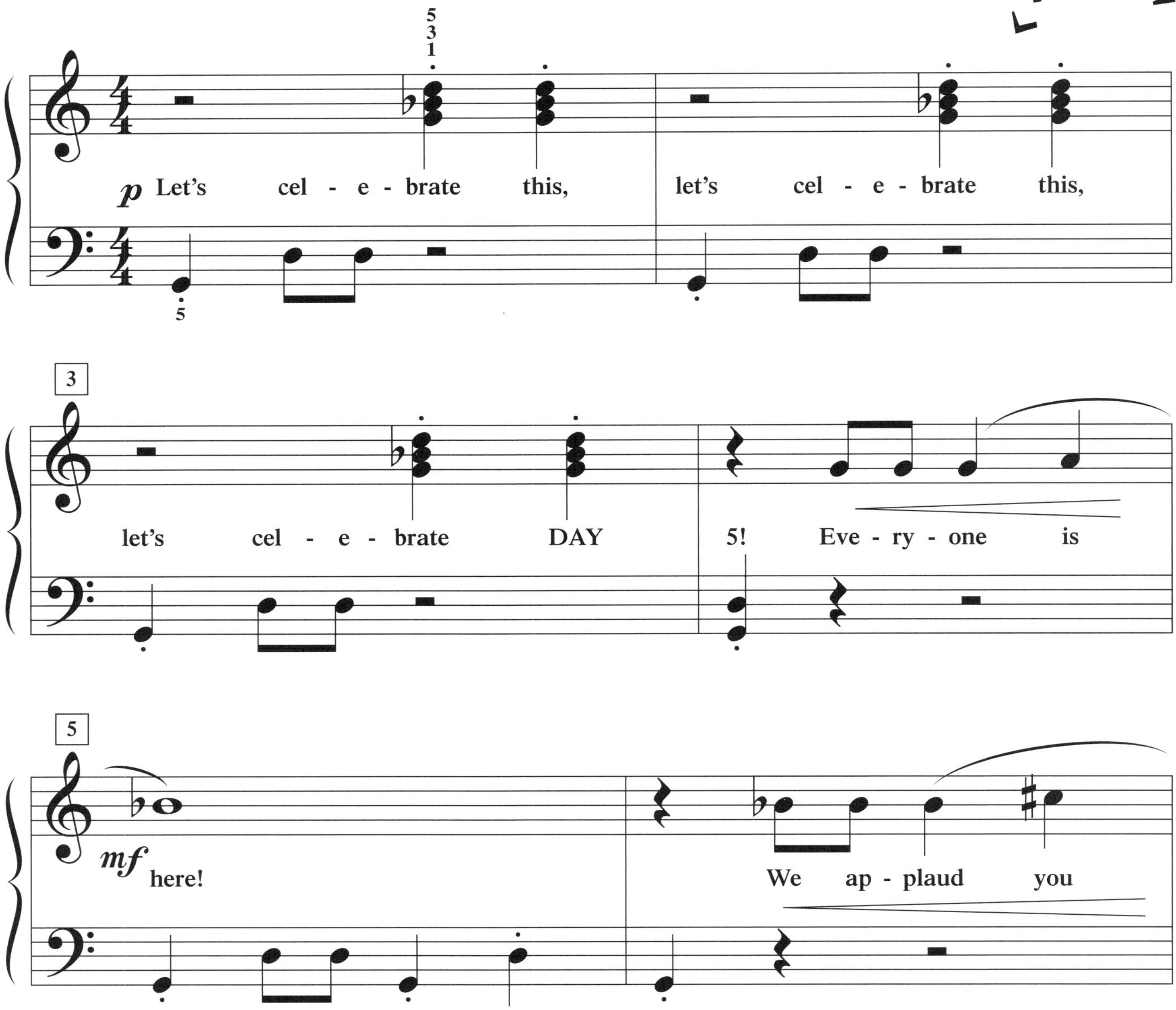
5
3
1
p Let's cel - e - brate this, let's cel - e - brate this,
5
3
let's cel - e - brate DAY 5! Eve - ry - one is
5
mf here! We ap - plaud you

7
now.
You have sight - read,
9
sight - read, sight - read,
man - y notes and now you're
11
done.
Now you're done.
GREAT!
WELL DONE, SIGHTREADER!
VIVALDI

Piano Adventures® Certificate

CONGRATULATIONS

____

(Your Name)

You are now a Level 2A Sightreader. Keep up the great work!

____

Teacher Date